# Illuminating Magic

MADAME OPHELIA

# CONTENTS

# THE POWER
# OF CANDLE MAGIC

**W**elcome to the enchanting world of candle magic! In this book, we will explore the profound and transformative practice of harnessing the power of candles within the sacred tradition of Wicca.

Candle magic is a cornerstone of Wiccan spellwork, revered for its ability to manifest intentions, channel energies, and connect with the divine. The simple act of lighting a candle can ignite a profound transformation within ourselves and our surroundings. Through the flickering flame, we tap into the ancient wisdom of our ancestors and commune with the forces of nature.

Within these pages, we will delve into the profound significance of candle magic in the realm of Wicca. We will learn about the symbolic language of colors and the correspondences that align with different intentions. We will discover the various types of candles and how to choose the perfect candle for our spells.

But candle magic is not merely about lighting a candle and reciting a few words. It is a deeply personal and spiritual practice that requires reverence, intention, and focus. We will explore the importance of creating a sacred space and preparing ourselves mentally, emotionally, and energetically before engaging in candle spellwork. Ethical considerations will also be discussed, as Wiccans value the principles of harm none and respect for the free will of all beings.

Throughout this journey, we will uncover the foundational aspects of candle magic, guiding you through basic spells for love, protection, healing, prosperity, divination, and more. As your understanding deepens, we will embark on more advanced practices, such as working with the elements, lunar and solar energies, ancestral connections, and celebrating the cycles of the Wheel of the Year.

While this book serves as a guide, it is essential to remember that the true power of candle magic lies within your own intuition and connection with the divine. As you immerse yourself in the rituals and ceremonies within these pages, always trust your inner knowing and adapt the practices to suit your unique path.

So, kindle the flame of curiosity within your heart, and let the magic of candle spells illuminate your journey through the ancient wisdom of Wicca. May you find inspiration, transformation, and a deeper connection to the mystical realms as we embark on this enchanting exploration together. Blessed be!

# BRIEF HISTORY OF CANDLE MAGIC IN WICCA

To understand the significance of candle magic in Wicca, we must delve into its rich historical roots and explore its evolution within the practice. Candle magic has been intertwined with spiritual traditions throughout human history, serving as a potent tool for rituals, divination, and spellcasting.

In the context of Wicca, candle magic has deep connections to the beliefs and practices of the Craft. Wicca itself emerged in the mid-20th century, influenced by ancient pagan beliefs, ceremonial magic, and folk traditions. Within this modern spiritual movement, the use of candles as a focal point for magical work has become an integral part of ritual practices.

The practice of candle magic traces its origins back to ancient times, when it was prevalent in various cultures and spiritual systems. The use of candles in religious rites and ceremonies can be found in ancient Egypt, Greece, Rome, and other civilizations. Candles were seen as a way to invoke and honor deities, offer prayers, and seek guidance from the divine.

Within Wicca, the use of candles gained prominence with the revival of witchcraft in the 20th century. Influential figures such as Gerald Gardner and Doreen Valiente, instrumental in the development and popularization of modern Wicca, incorporated candle magic as a central component of their practices.

Candles hold deep symbolism in Wiccan spirituality. The flickering flame represents the element of fire, a potent force of transformation, passion, and illumination. The colors of candles are carefully chosen to align with specific intentions and correspondences, such as red for love, green for prosperity, or white for purity and protection.

In Wiccan rituals and spellcasting, candles serve as a focal point, amplifying intention and directing energy. The act of lighting a candle, infusing it with intention, and allowing it to burn through a ritual or spell is seen as a powerful way to manifest desires, connect with the divine, and create positive change in one's life.

Over the years, candle magic in Wicca has evolved and diversified, with practitioners exploring various techniques, rituals, and correspondences. From basic spells for everyday purposes to intricate ceremonial practices aligned with the Wheel of the Year, candle magic remains a versatile and accessible tool for Wiccans seeking to manifest their intentions and deepen their spiritual connection.

As we journey through the pages of this book, we will honor and draw upon the historical foundations of candle magic in Wicca while embracing our own intuitive understanding and personal experiences. Through the ancient wisdom and contemporary practice of candle magic, we continue to kindle the flame of tradition and forge our unique path within the ever-evolving tapestry of Wiccan spirituality.

# PREPARING FOR CANDLE MAGIC

Before delving into the realm of candle magic, it is essential to prepare yourself and create a sacred space that supports your intentions and connects you with the energies of the divine. Preparation is a vital aspect of any magical practice, allowing you to align your mind, body, and spirit with the work ahead.

1. Clearing and Cleansing: Begin by clearing and cleansing your space. This can be done through various methods such as smudging with sage or using consecrated water. Clearing away any negative or stagnant energy creates a fresh and receptive environment for your candle magic.

2. Meditation and Grounding: Take a few moments to center yourself through meditation or grounding exercises. This helps to calm the

mind, focus your intention, and establish a strong connection with the Earth and the spiritual energies around you. Visualize yourself rooted to the ground, drawing in the supportive and nurturing energy of the Earth.

3. Gathering Supplies: Collect the necessary supplies for your candle magic ritual. This may include candles of appropriate colors, matches or a lighter, holders or candlesticks, essential oils or herbs for anointing, and any other tools or symbols that resonate with your intention.

4. Choosing the Right Candle: Select a candle that aligns with the purpose of your spell or ritual. Consider the color symbolism and correspondences associated with various intentions. For example, a green candle may be chosen for abundance and prosperity, while a pink candle may be used for matters of love and healing. Intuitively choose the candle that resonates with your desired outcome.

5. Anointing and Charging: Anointing the candle with oils or herbs is a powerful way to infuse it with your intention. Select oils or herbs that correspond to your desired outcome and rub them onto the candle while visualizing your in-

tention. As you do so, imbue the candle with your energy and purpose.

6. Setting Sacred Space: Create a sacred space for your candle magic ritual. This can be done by casting a circle, either physically or through visualization, to create a sacred and protected area. Invoke the elements, deities, or spirits that resonate with your practice and seek their guidance and blessings.

7. Setting Intentions: Clarify your intention for the candle magic ritual. Clearly state what you wish to manifest or achieve, keeping it focused and specific. Write down your intention on a piece of paper or hold it clearly in your mind as you proceed.

8. Lighting the Candle: Light the candle with reverence and intention. As the flame ignites, visualize your intention manifesting and feel the energy of your purpose flowing into the candle. Focus your thoughts and emotions on the desired outcome.

9. Ritual or Spellwork: Engage in your chosen ritual or spellwork. This may involve reciting affirmations or incantations, performing specific actions, or simply sitting in quiet contempla-

tion. Allow the candle to burn, symbolizing the release of your intention into the universe.

10. Closing and Gratitude: Once your ritual or spellwork is complete, express gratitude to the divine forces, elements, and spirits that have been present with you. Thank them for their guidance, assistance, and the energy they have provided. Close your sacred space by releasing the circle, acknowledging the completion of your candle magic.

By preparing yourself and your space in these ways, you set the foundation for a focused and potent candle magic practice. Remember to trust your intuition, follow your heart, and adapt these steps to suit your personal preferences and spiritual path. With dedication, intention, and a clear connection to the energies around you, your candle magic rituals will become profound gateways to transformation and manifestation.

# ETHICAL CONSIDERATIONS IN CANDLE SPELLWORK

E thics and responsibility are fundamental aspects of Wicca and should be carefully considered when engaging in candle spellwork. Wiccans follow the principle of "harm none" and hold a deep respect for the free will and well-being of all beings. When working with candle magic, it is crucial to uphold these ethical considerations. Here are some key points to keep in mind:

1. Respect for Free Will: Always ensure that your candle spells and intentions align with the principles of respect and free will. It is essential to avoid manipulating or coercing the thoughts, emotions, or actions of others through your spellwork. Focus on manifesting positive change in your own life rather than at-

tempting to control or influence the lives of others without their consent.

2. Intentions of Benevolence: Direct your intentions towards positive outcomes and benevolent purposes. Seek to manifest love, healing, protection, abundance, and personal growth. Avoid using candle magic to cause harm, seek revenge, or engage in negative actions. Work towards the highest good for yourself and others.

3. Consideration of Consequences: Before performing any candle spell, carefully consider the potential consequences and effects of your actions. Reflect on the long-term implications of your intentions and ensure that they align with your values and the well-being of all involved. Take responsibility for the ripple effects of your spellwork.

4. Permission and Consent: When performing candle magic on behalf of others, it is crucial to obtain their explicit permission and consent. Respect their autonomy and allow them to make their own choices. It is not ethical to perform spellwork on someone without their knowledge or consent.

5. Environmental Awareness: Be mindful of the impact of your candle magic on the environment. Opt for sustainable and eco-friendly candles, such as those made from natural and biodegradable materials. Avoid excessive use of resources and dispose of candles and associated materials responsibly.

6. Clear Intention and Clarity of Purpose: Maintain a clear and focused intention when working with candle spells. Ensure that your purpose is aligned with your highest values and the ethical framework of Wicca. Take the time to reflect on your intentions and ensure they are rooted in positivity and integrity.

7. Karmic Awareness: Understand and respect the concept of karma. Recognize that the energy you put out into the world will come back to you. Approach candle spellwork with honesty, integrity, and a genuine desire to create positive change. Practice self-reflection and take responsibility for your actions and intentions.

By embracing these ethical considerations, you align your candle spellwork with the principles of Wicca and cultivate a practice that is in harmony with the greater good. Remember, as a practitioner of Wicca, you have the power to manifest change while upholding respect, compassion, and ethical responsibility.

# TYPES OF CANDLES AND THEIR SIGNIFICANCE

I n candle magic, the type of candle you choose holds symbolic significance and can enhance the energy and intention of your spellwork. Each type of candle possesses unique qualities and correspondences that align with specific purposes and intentions. Here are some common types of candles used in Wiccan practices and their associated significance:

1. Taper Candles: Taper candles are long, slender candles often used in rituals and ceremonies. They represent the element of fire and are commonly associated with the power of transformation, illumination, and spiritual awakening. Taper candles are versatile and can be used for various intentions depending on their color.

2. Chime Candles: Chime candles are small, thin candles that come in a variety of colors. They are typically used for shorter spells or rituals and are ideal for focusing on specific intentions. Chime candles can be easily found in Wiccan supply stores and are a popular choice for practitioners.

3. Pillar Candles: Pillar candles are thick, cylindrical candles that provide a steady and long-lasting burn. They symbolize strength, stability, and endurance. Pillar candles are often used for spells and rituals that require sustained energy or for creating a sacred and welcoming atmosphere.

4. Votive Candles: Votive candles are small, usually round candles that are contained in a cup or holder. They are designed to burn for several hours and are commonly used for prayers, devotion, and meditation. Votive candles are often used to invoke specific deities or to create a sacred ambiance during rituals.

5. Jar Candles: Jar candles are candles placed in glass jars or containers, allowing them to burn safely and for longer durations. They are versatile and can be found in various sizes and colors. Jar candles are frequently used for spells

and rituals related to protection, healing, and manifestation.

6. Tea Light Candles: Tea light candles are small, shallow candles that come in metal or plastic cups. They are convenient, easy to use, and burn for a shorter period. Tea light candles are popular for creating an ambient atmosphere or for quick and simple candle spells.

7. Figure Candles: Figure candles are shaped like human figures or specific symbols and are often used for more intricate and personalized spellwork. They can be carved or inscribed with sigils, names, or intentions to enhance the focus and energy of the spell.

8. Elemental Candles: Elemental candles represent the four elements of nature—fire, air, water, and earth. These candles are often used to invoke and connect with the elemental energies during rituals or spellwork. The colors associated with each element can be used to enhance the corresponding intentions.

9. Zodiac Candles: Zodiac candles are associated with astrological signs and are used to align with specific energies or to enhance spellwork related to astrological influences. These candles can be used in rituals or spellwork during spe-

cific zodiac seasons or to tap into the qualities associated with each sign.

10. Intentionally Crafted Candles: Intentionally crafted candles are handmade candles infused with specific oils, herbs, or crystals to align with particular intentions. These candles are carefully crafted by practitioners or artisans, focusing on the energetic properties and correspondences of the chosen ingredients.

When selecting a candle for your spellwork, consider the color symbolism, the purpose of your ritual, and your personal connection to the energy of the candle. Trust your intuition and choose the candle that resonates with your intention and the desired outcome. By understanding the significance of different types of candles, you can enhance the potency and effectiveness of your candle magic practice.

# COLORS AND CORRESPONDENCES

I n candle magic, the color of the candle holds symbolic significance and can enhance the energy and intention of your spellwork. Each color has its own unique vibrations and correspondences that align with specific purposes and intentions. Understanding the meanings associated with different colors will allow you to select the most appropriate candle for your desired outcome. Here are some common colors used in candle magic and their correspondences:

1. White: White candles symbolize purity, spirituality, and clarity. They are often used for rituals involving purification, healing, protection, and spiritual guidance. White candles are also suitable for any intention when you desire to bring balance and harmony into your life.

2. Red: Red candles represent passion, love, courage, and strength. They are commonly used in spells related to matters of the heart, sexuality, vitality, and personal power. Red candles can also be used for energizing and activating intentions that require motivation and assertiveness.

3. Pink: Pink candles embody love, romance, compassion, and emotional healing. They are often used in spells aimed at attracting love, fostering self-love and acceptance, and mending relationships. Pink candles carry a gentle and nurturing energy that promotes harmony and emotional well-being.

4. Green: Green candles symbolize abundance, prosperity, growth, and fertility. They are commonly used in spells and rituals associated with financial prosperity, career success, and healing the physical body. Green candles also connect with the energy of nature and can be used to promote harmony with the environment.

5. Blue: Blue candles represent peace, tranquility, communication, and spiritual awareness. They are used in spells and rituals related to emotional healing, intuition, psychic abilities, and

enhancing spiritual connections. Blue candles can also be used for invoking protection and promoting serenity.

6. Yellow: Yellow candles embody joy, intellect, clarity, and creativity. They are often used in spells and rituals focused on enhancing mental abilities, boosting confidence, and manifesting new ideas or opportunities. Yellow candles bring a vibrant and uplifting energy to spell-work.

7. Orange: Orange candles symbolize enthusiasm, energy, creativity, and manifestation. They are commonly used in spells related to career success, motivation, and attracting opportunities. Orange candles also resonate with the energy of the Sun, bringing warmth, vitality, and positivity to spellwork.

8. Purple: Purple candles represent spirituality, psychic abilities, intuition, and spiritual awakening. They are often used in spells aimed at enhancing spiritual growth, accessing higher realms, and connecting with divine guidance. Purple candles carry mystical and transformative energy.

9. Black: Black candles symbolize protection, banishing negativity, and warding off negative en-

ergies. They are used in spells aimed at breaking bad habits, releasing attachments, and removing obstacles. Black candles can also be used for deep meditation and introspection.

10. Silver: Silver candles embody feminine energy, intuition, and lunar magic. They are used in spells and rituals related to psychic development, divination, and invoking the energy of the Moon. Silver candles bring a sense of fluidity and receptivity to spellwork.

11. Gold: Gold candles symbolize wealth, success, abundance, and prosperity. They are commonly used in spells and rituals focused on financial growth, career advancement, and attracting abundance in all areas of life. Gold candles carry a radiant and empowering energy.

Remember that these color correspondences serve as general guidelines, but personal associations and cultural variations can also influence their meanings. Trust your intuition and connect with the energy of the colors that resonate with you the most. By utilizing the power of colors in candle magic, you can amplify your intentions and align your spellwork with specific aspects of life and energy.

Regenerate response

# SELECTING THE RIGHT CANDLE FOR YOUR SPELLS

C hoosing the right candle for your spells is essential in candle magic. The color, size, and shape of the candle can significantly influence the energy and effectiveness of your spellwork. Here are some factors to consider when selecting the perfect candle for your spells:

1.  Intention and Purpose: Clarify the intention and purpose of your spell. Determine the outcome you wish to manifest or the energy you want to attract. Each candle color holds its own unique symbolism and correspondence. Refer to the color correspondences section to find the color that aligns best with your desired intention.

2.  Candle Size and Shape: Consider the size and shape of the candle based on the type of spell

or ritual you are performing. Taper candles are ideal for longer rituals or when you want the candle to burn for an extended period. Chime or votive candles are suitable for shorter spells or when you desire a quicker burn. Figure candles or shaped candles can add a personalized touch to your spellwork.

3. Candle Quality: Opt for high-quality candles made from natural materials, such as beeswax or soy wax. These candles burn cleaner and emit less smoke. Avoid candles with synthetic additives or strong scents that may interfere with the energy of your spellwork.

4. Candle Preparation: Some practitioners prefer to consecrate or charge their candles before using them in spells. This involves infusing the candle with your intention and energy. You can anoint the candle with oils, carve symbols or sigils into it, or bless it with your intention through visualization and focused energy.

5. Candle Safety: Ensure that the candle you choose is safe for the specific spell or ritual you plan to perform. Consider factors such as burn time, the availability of a secure holder, and any fire safety precautions you need to take.

Safety should always be a top priority when working with candles.

6. Personal Connection: Trust your intuition and personal connection when selecting a candle. If a particular candle catches your eye or resonates with you on an intuitive level, it may be the perfect choice. Your intuition can guide you in finding the candle that will best support your intentions.

Remember, while the color of the candle is significant, it is not the only factor to consider. Take into account other aspects such as the candle's size, shape, quality, and safety. Also, be open to experimenting and adapting based on your own experiences and preferences.

By carefully selecting the right candle for your spells, you align the energy and symbolism of the candle with your intention, amplifying the effectiveness of your candle magic. Trust your instincts, be mindful of the correspondences, and enjoy the process of exploring the diverse and enchanting world of candle magic.

# CLEANSING AND CHARGING CANDLES

Before using candles in your spellwork, it is important to cleanse and charge them to align them with your intentions and remove any unwanted energies. Cleansing and charging candles help to enhance their potency and ensure that they are attuned to your specific spell or ritual. Here are some methods for cleansing and charging candles:

1. Sunlight or Moonlight: Place your candles in direct sunlight or moonlight for a few hours to cleanse and recharge them. The sunlight or moonlight will help clear any negative or stagnant energies accumulated in the candles, infusing them with fresh energy and vitality. Moonlight, in particular, is often associated with feminine energy and can add a gentle and nurturing essence to your candles.

2. Elemental Cleansing: Pass your candles through the smoke of incense or hold them near the element of air (such as waving them gently in the breeze) to cleanse them. You can also sprinkle a few drops of water on the candles or lightly mist them to symbolically cleanse them with the element of water. Alternatively, burying the candles in the earth for a short period can ground and purify their energy.

3. Visualization and Intention: Hold the candles in your hands and visualize a stream of pure, cleansing energy flowing through them. Envision any unwanted energies dissipating and the candles becoming vibrant and charged with positive energy. State your intention aloud or silently, directing your focused energy into the candles.

4. Sound Cleansing: Use sound to cleanse your candles by ringing a bell or using a singing bowl near them. The vibrations produced by the sound will help clear away any stagnant or discordant energies, leaving the candles energetically cleansed and refreshed.

5. Crystal Cleansing: Surround your candles with crystals known for their cleansing properties,

such as clear quartz, selenite, or amethyst. Leave the candles in close proximity to the crystals for a period of time, allowing the crystals' energies to cleanse and purify the candles.

6. Ritual Bath: Immerse your candles in a solution of salt water or herbal-infused water, such as rosemary or lavender. As you submerge the candles, visualize the water purifying and cleansing them, washing away any negative energies. After the bath, gently pat the candles dry.

Remember to use methods that resonate with you personally and align with your own practice. Trust your intuition and adapt the cleansing and charging process to suit your individual preferences.

By cleansing and charging your candles, you create a sacred and attuned tool for your spellwork. This process helps to remove any energetic blockages and ensures that your candles are infused with the purest intentions, allowing their magic to unfold with greater potency and effectiveness.

# CREATING
# A SACRED SPACE

Creating a sacred space is an essential step in Wiccan practices, including candle magic. Sacred space provides a dedicated and energetically attuned environment where you can focus your intentions, connect with the divine, and perform your rituals or spellwork. Here are some steps to help you create a sacred space for your candle magic:

1. Intention Setting: Begin by setting your intention for the sacred space. Clarify the purpose of the space, whether it is for meditation, spellcasting, or spiritual connection. Align your intention with creating a space that feels safe, sacred, and conducive to your practice.

2. Cleanse the Space: Before creating your sacred space, cleanse the area to remove any stagnant or negative energies. You can use methods

such as smudging with sage or other cleansing herbs, sprinkling salt water, or using sound vibrations from a singing bowl or bell. Visualize the space being purified and cleared as you perform the cleansing ritual.

3. Arrange Altar or Sacred Items: Set up an altar or a designated area where you can place your candles, ritual tools, and other sacred items. Choose items that hold personal significance to you, such as crystals, statues, symbols, or representations of the elements. Arrange them in a way that feels visually appealing and energetically meaningful to you.

4. Select Decor and Ambiance: Enhance the ambiance of your sacred space by adding decorative elements that resonate with your practice. Consider using colors, fabrics, candles, flowers, or artwork that evoke a sense of peace, harmony, and spiritual connection. Choose items that align with your personal aesthetic and create an atmosphere that supports your intentions.

5. Set Sacred Space Boundaries: Use physical or energetic boundaries to demarcate your sacred space. You can create a physical boundary using a designated rug, cloth, or a circle of stones. Alternatively, visualize an energetic boundary

by mentally drawing a circle or envisioning a sphere of protective energy around your space. This boundary acts as a container for your energy and intentions.

6. Cleanse and Charge the Space: Once the physical space is prepared, cleanse and charge the energy within the sacred space. You can use methods such as visualization, incense, or sound vibrations to infuse the space with positive energy and intention. Walk around the perimeter of the space, focusing your attention on each direction (north, east, south, west) and invoking the energies associated with them.

7. Sacred Space Ritual: Create a simple ritual to consecrate and dedicate your sacred space. Light a candle or incense, express gratitude to the divine or your chosen deities, and state your intention for the space. You can recite a prayer, chant, or affirmations that resonate with your spiritual path. Allow yourself to connect deeply with the energy of the space and the sacredness of the moment.

Remember that the creation of a sacred space is a personal and evolving process. It is important to regularly cleanse, maintain, and refresh your sacred space to keep its energy aligned with your intentions and practice. Trust your intuition and adapt the steps to suit your own spiritual journey.

By creating a sacred space for your candle magic, you establish a dedicated and energetically attuned environment that supports and amplifies your intentions and spellwork. This space becomes a sanctuary where you can connect with the divine, access higher realms, and work your magic with focused intention and reverence.

# CHOOSING RITUAL TOOLS FOR CANDLE MAGIC

Ritual tools can enhance your candle magic practice, allowing you to focus your energy, direct your intentions, and create a sacred connection with the divine. While not all tools are necessary, incorporating them can deepen your connection to the rituals and amplify the effectiveness of your spellwork. Here are some common ritual tools used in candle magic:

1. Athame: An athame is a ceremonial knife with a double-edged blade. It represents the element of Fire and is used to direct energy, carve symbols on candles, or cast a sacred circle. The athame is a symbol of willpower and is often associated with masculine energy.

2. Chalice: A chalice is a ritual cup that represents the element of Water. It can be used to hold

consecrated water, wine, or other sacred liquids. The chalice symbolizes the divine feminine, intuition, and emotions. It is often used for libations or as a tool for offering.

3. Wand: A wand is a slender, handheld tool that represents the element of Air. It is used to direct energy, draw symbols in the air, or cast circles. Wands can be made from various materials such as wood, crystal, or metal. They symbolize intention, focus, and the power of manifestation.

4. Pentacle: A pentacle is a disc or plate inscribed with a five-pointed star within a circle. It represents the element of Earth and is a symbol of protection, grounding, and manifestation. The pentacle can be used as a base for placing candles or other objects during rituals.

5. Censer: A censer, also known as a thurible, is a container used for burning incense. It symbolizes the element of Air and is used to purify the space, enhance ritual ambiance, and carry prayers or intentions through the smoke. The censer represents the connection between the physical and spiritual realms.

6. Bell: A bell is a tool used to mark significant moments in rituals or to create sacred sound

vibrations. It can be rung at the beginning and end of a ritual, to call in specific energies, or to signify transitions. The bell is believed to clear stagnant energy and attract positive vibrations.

7. Besom: A besom is a broomstick typically made from natural materials such as twigs and branches. It symbolizes the element of Air and is used to cleanse and purify the ritual space by sweeping away negative energy. The besom is also associated with protection and can be used to create energetic boundaries.

8. Incense: Incense is used to add fragrance and create an atmosphere conducive to ritual and spiritual practices. Different types of incense have their own correspondences and can be selected based on their energetic properties. Common types include frankincense, sage, lavender, or sandalwood.

Remember that these ritual tools are not mandatory, and your practice can be just as effective without them. Choose the tools that resonate with you and align with your intentions. Personalize your tools by selecting ones that hold personal significance or that you feel drawn to.

By incorporating ritual tools into your candle magic practice, you infuse your rituals with symbolism, intention, and focused energy. These tools can serve as reminders of your connection to the divine, aid in your visualization and intention-setting, and create a sacred atmosphere that enhances the power of your spellwork.

# TIMING AND ASTROLOGICAL CONSIDERATIONS

Timing plays a significant role in candle magic, as certain days, phases of the moon, and astrological alignments can enhance the energy and effectiveness of your spellwork. By aligning your candle magic with the natural rhythms and energetic influences of the universe, you can harness additional power and increase the potency of your intentions. Here are some timing and astrological considerations to keep in mind:

1. Days of the Week: Each day of the week is associated with specific planetary energy, which can influence the outcome of your spellwork. Consider the correspondences below when choosing the day to perform your candle magic:

- o Sunday: Associated with the Sun and is ideal for spells related to success, vitality, and confidence.
- o Monday: Aligned with the Moon and is suitable for spells focused on emotions, intuition, and feminine energy.
- o Tuesday: Ruled by Mars and is conducive to spells for courage, strength, and protection.
- o Wednesday: Associated with Mercury and is favorable for spells related to communication, intellect, and divination.
- o Thursday: Ruled by Jupiter and is ideal for spells focused on abundance, growth, and expansion.
- o Friday: Aligned with Venus and is suited for spells related to love, beauty, and relationships.
- o Saturday: Associated with Saturn and is favorable for spells for grounding, protection, and banishing.

2. Moon Phases: The phases of the moon carry their own unique energies that can amplify specific intentions in your candle magic. Con-

sider the following moon phases when planning your spellwork:

- o New Moon: Represents beginnings, manifestation, and setting intentions.
- o Waxing Moon: Ideal for spells focused on growth, attraction, and abundance.
- o Full Moon: Symbolizes peak energy, completion, and manifestation.
- o Waning Moon: Suitable for spells related to release, banishing, and letting go.

3. Planetary Hours: Each day is divided into planetary hours, which correspond to the different planets. These hours can align with specific intentions or planetary energies. Use a planetary hour calculator to determine the ideal hour for your candle magic based on the planet associated with your intention.

4. Retrogrades: Take note of any significant planetary retrogrades that might be occurring during your spellwork. Retrogrades can impact the energy and flow of your intentions. Some practitioners choose to avoid spellcasting during retrogrades, while others work with retrograde energies for introspection, release, or review.

5. Personal Astrological Chart: Consider your own astrological chart when planning your candle magic. Your birth chart can provide insights into your strengths, weaknesses, and areas of focus. Aligning your intentions with your astrological influences can create a powerful synergy between your personal energy and the cosmic energies at play.

6. Intuition and Synchronicity: Ultimately, trust your intuition and pay attention to synchronicities. If you feel a strong pull to perform your candle magic on a particular day or during a specific astrological alignment, honor that intuitive guidance. The universe often communicates with us through signs and synchronicities, guiding us to the optimal timing for our spellwork.

Remember, while timing and astrological considerations can enhance your candle magic, they are not the sole determinants of its success. Your intentions, focus, and energy play a vital role in the effectiveness of your spells. Adapt these timing considerations to suit your personal practice and trust your own intuitive guidance.

By aligning your candle magic with the natural rhythms of the universe, you tap into the energetic currents that support and amplify your intentions. Working with the planetary influences and timing considerations enhances the potency of your spell-work, creating a deeper connection to the cosmic forces at play.

# CASTING THE CIRCLE

C asting a circle is a fundamental practice in Wicca and many other magical traditions. The circle serves as a sacred space, a boundary between the mundane and the spiritual realms, and a container for your energy and intentions during your candle magic rituals. Here is a step-by-step guide to casting the circle:

1. Preparation: Choose a quiet and undisturbed space for your ritual. Cleanse the area, ensuring it is free from clutter and distractions. Gather your ritual tools, candles, and any other items you will need for your spellwork.

2. Centering and Grounding: Begin by centering yourself and grounding your energy. Take a few deep breaths, allowing yourself to become present and focused. Visualize roots extending from your feet into the earth, grounding you

and connecting you with the energy of the earth.

3. Purification: Before casting the circle, purify the space and yourself. You can do this by smudging the area with sage or other cleansing herbs, sprinkling salt water around the perimeter, or using sound vibrations to clear the energy.

4. Opening the Circle: Starting in the East, take your wand or athame and visualize a beam of energy extending from the tool as you move clockwise around the perimeter of the circle. As you walk, envision a shimmering, protective barrier forming around the space. As you return to the East, complete the circle, connecting the beginning and end points.

5. Calling the Quarters: Stand in the center of the circle facing East. Hold your wand or athame pointed upward. Call upon the energies associated with each direction:

   o East: Invoke the element of Air and its qualities of communication, intellect, and inspiration. Welcome the energies of the East and the spirits of the East to join your circle.
   o South: Invoke the element of Fire and its qualities of passion, transformation, and

willpower. Welcome the energies of the South and the spirits of the South to join your circle.

o West: Invoke the element of Water and its qualities of emotions, intuition, and healing. Welcome the energies of the West and the spirits of the West to join your circle.

o North: Invoke the element of Earth and its qualities of stability, grounding, and abundance. Welcome the energies of the North and the spirits of the North to join your circle.

6. Statement of Purpose: State your intention for casting the circle and your spellwork. Express your gratitude for the elements and the spirits that have joined your circle, acknowledging their presence and assistance.

7. Ritual Work: Proceed with your candle magic ritual, spellcasting, or any other practices you have planned within the sacred space of the circle. Focus your energy, direct your intentions, and connect with the divine energies.

8. Closing the Circle: Once you have completed your ritual work, it is time to close the circle. Begin in the North, holding your wand or

athame pointed downward. Move counter-clockwise around the perimeter of the circle, visualizing the energy of the circle being drawn back into your tool. As you return to the North, complete the circle, severing the connection and closing the energetic boundary.

9. Gratitude and Farewell: Offer gratitude to the elements, the spirits, and any deities or divine beings you have called upon. Express your appreciation for their presence and assistance. Take a moment to ground yourself and release any excess energy that may remain.

Casting the circle creates a sacred and protected space for your candle magic. It allows you to work in harmony with the energies of the elements and the divine, establishing a focused and powerful environment for your rituals. Remember to adapt the circle-casting process to suit your personal practice and preferences.

By casting the circle, you create a consecrated space that amplifies your energy and intentions, ensuring a heightened and sacred experience during your candle magic rituals.

# LOVE AND ATTRACTION SPELLS

L ove and attraction spells are a common aspect of candle magic, allowing individuals to manifest love, enhance existing relationships, or attract romantic partners. These spells harness the power of intention, symbolism, and focused energy to create positive shifts in matters of the heart. Here are some love and attraction spells you can practice with candles:

1. Attracting Love Spell:

   o Choose a pink or red candle, symbolizing love and passion.
   o Carve symbols or words that represent love and attraction onto the candle.
   o Anoint the candle with a love-drawing oil, such as rose or jasmine oil.

- Light the candle and visualize yourself surrounded by loving and supportive energy.
- Focus on the qualities you desire in a partner and the loving relationship you wish to attract.
- Allow the candle to burn completely, releasing your intentions to the universe.

2. Rekindling Romance Spell:

- Select a red or orange candle to represent passion and desire.
- Carve your and your partner's initials or names onto the candle.
- Anoint the candle with sensual oil, such as ylang-ylang or patchouli oil.
- Light the candle and visualize the flame reigniting the spark of love and passion in your relationship.
- Send loving and positive energy to your partner, envisioning a deep connection and renewed romance.
- Let the candle burn for a specific period each day until it is extinguished.

3. Self-Love Spell:

- Choose a pink or white candle, representing self-love and inner peace.
- Carve empowering affirmations or symbols onto the candle.
- Anoint the candle with a nurturing oil, such as lavender or chamomile oil.
- Light the candle and focus on cultivating a deep sense of self-love and acceptance.
- Release any negative self-perceptions and embrace your worthiness of love and happiness.
- Allow the candle to burn completely, absorbing the loving energy you have invoked.

4. Friendship and Social Connections Spell:

- Select a green or yellow candle to symbolize friendship and social connections.
- Carve symbols or words that represent friendship onto the candle.
- Anoint the candle with a socializing oil, such as bergamot or lemon oil.
- Light the candle and visualize yourself surrounded by a supportive and uplifting social circle.

- Imagine meeting new friends or strengthening existing friendships, fostering harmonious connections.
- Let the candle burn for a specific period each day until it is extinguished.

Remember to always approach love and attraction spells with respect and a focus on the highest good for all involved. Be mindful of free will and ethical considerations, ensuring that your intentions align with the principles of love, compassion, and consent.

Candle magic spells can serve as powerful tools for manifesting love and attraction in your life. By infusing your intentions into the flame, you tap into the universal energy and invite positive shifts in your romantic experiences. As with any spellwork, trust your intuition and adjust the spells to suit your specific needs and preferences.

# PROTECTION AND BANISHING SPELLS

Protection and banishing spells are essential aspects of candle magic, allowing practitioners to create energetic boundaries, ward off negativity, and remove unwanted influences from their lives. These spells utilize the power of intention, visualization, and focused energy to safeguard against harm and create a sense of security. Here are some protection and banishing spells you can practice with candles:

1. Shielding and Protection Spell:

    o Choose a black or white candle, symbolizing protection and purification.
    o Carve protective symbols, such as a pentacle or a personal sigil, onto the candle.
    o Anoint the candle with protective oil, such as frankincense or myrrh oil.

- Light the candle and visualize a brilliant, protective shield forming around you.
- See this shield repelling negative energy, warding off harm, and keeping you safe.
- Allow the candle to burn completely, sealing your protective intentions.

2. Banishing Negative Energy Spell:

- Select a black candle to represent the absorption and removal of negative energy.
- Carve symbols or words that represent banishing onto the candle.
- Anoint the candle with a purifying oil, such as sage or cedarwood oil.
- Light the candle and visualize the flame burning away and transforming negative energy into light.
- Focus on releasing any negativity, attachments, or unwanted influences from your life.
- Let the candle burn down completely, visualizing the space being cleared and purified.

3. Warding and Boundaries Spell:

- Choose a white or blue candle, symbolizing clarity and protection.
- Carve symbols or words that represent boundaries onto the candle.
- Anoint the candle with a boundary-setting oil, such as rosemary or basil oil.
- Light the candle and visualize a protective boundary forming around your home or personal space.
- See this boundary as impenetrable to any negative or harmful energies.
- Allow the candle to burn for a specific period each day until it is extinguished, reinforcing the protective boundaries.

4. Breaking Unhealthy Attachments Spell:

- Select a black or gray candle to represent the severing of unhealthy attachments.
- Carve the name or symbol of the attachment onto the candle.
- Anoint the candle with a releasing oil, such as lemon or eucalyptus oil.
- Light the candle and visualize the flame burning away the energetic cords that bind you.

- ○ Focus on releasing any emotional or energetic ties that no longer serve your highest good.
- ○ Let the candle burn down completely, symbolizing the complete release and freedom from unhealthy attachments.

When performing protection and banishing spells, it is important to set clear intentions, work with focused energy, and approach the spells with respect and caution. Remember to consider the ethical implications of your actions and to work in alignment with the principles of harm none.

Candle magic spells for protection and banishing provide a powerful means to create energetic boundaries, remove negativity, and promote a sense of safety and well-being. Adapt these spells to suit your personal beliefs and preferences, and trust your intuition as you work with the energy of the candles.

# HEALING AND WELLNESS SPELLS

Healing and wellness spells are a powerful way to enhance physical, emotional, and spiritual well-being through the practice of candle magic. These spells harness the energy of candles, intention, and visualization to promote healing, restore balance, and support overall wellness. Here are some healing and wellness spells you can practice with candles:

1. Physical Healing Spell:

    o Choose a green or blue candle, symbolizing healing and restoration.

    o Carve healing symbols or words onto the candle, such as the Caduceus or the word "healing."

    o Anoint the candle with healing oil, such as lavender or tea tree oil.

o Light the candle and visualize the flame as a source of healing energy.

o Direct this healing energy toward any areas of your body that require healing.

o See the energy soothing and nourishing the affected areas, promoting healing and well-being.

o Allow the candle to burn completely, symbolizing the completion of the healing process.

2. Emotional Healing Spell:

o Select a pink or yellow candle to represent emotional healing and upliftment.

o Carve symbols or words that symbolize emotional well-being onto the candle.

o Anoint the candle with an uplifting oil, such as rose or bergamot oil.

o Light the candle and visualize the flame as a source of soothing and healing energy.

o Focus on releasing any emotional pain, trauma, or negative emotions you may be carrying.

- See the healing energy enveloping you, bringing comfort, peace, and emotional balance.

- Let the candle burn down completely, symbolizing the release and healing of emotional wounds.

3. Spiritual Healing Spell:

- Choose a white or purple candle, representing spiritual purification and connection.

- Carve spiritual symbols or words onto the candle, such as a pentacle or the word "spiritual."

- Anoint the candle with a spiritual oil, such as frankincense or sandalwood oil.

- Light the candle and visualize the flame as a conduit for divine healing energy.

- Focus on opening yourself to receive spiritual healing and guidance.

- See the healing energy flowing through you, restoring your spiritual well-being and connection.

- Allow the candle to burn completely, symbolizing the integration of spiritual healing.

4. Overall Wellness Spell:

   o Select a candle color that resonates with your overall wellness goal, such as green for vitality or purple for balance.

   o Carve symbols or words onto the candle that represent your desired state of wellness.

   o Anoint the candle with oil that aligns with your wellness intention, such as eucalyptus or peppermint oil for rejuvenation.

   o Light the candle and visualize yourself in a state of optimal well-being.

   o See the energy of the flame infusing you with vitality, balance, or any other qualities you desire.

   o Let the candle burn for a specific period each day until it is extinguished, reinforcing your intention for overall wellness.

When practicing healing and wellness spells, it is important to approach them with a holistic mindset, considering the interconnectedness of mind, body, and spirit. These spells are not substitutes for medical or professional advice but can complement existing healing practices. Trust your intuition and adapt the spells to suit your specific needs and preferences.

Candle magic spells for healing and wellness provide a powerful means to promote physical, emotional, and spiritual well-being. Use them as tools for self-care, empowerment, and alignment with your highest state of wellness.

# PROSPERITY AND ABUNDANCE SPELLS

Prosperity and abundance spells are popular aspects of candle magic, allowing individuals to attract wealth, success, and material blessings into their lives. These spells harness the power of intention, visualization, and focused energy to align with the flow of abundance in the universe. Here are some prosperity and abundance spells you can practice with candles:

1. Wealth Attraction Spell:

    o Choose a green or gold candle, symbolizing wealth and prosperity.

    o Carve symbols or words representing abundance onto the candle.

    o Anoint the candle with a money-drawing oil, such as cinnamon or patchouli oil.

- Light the candle and visualize yourself surrounded by a golden aura of abundance.
- Focus on attracting financial opportunities and an abundant flow of wealth into your life.
- See yourself living a prosperous and abundant lifestyle.
- Allow the candle to burn completely, releasing your intentions to manifest wealth.

2. Career Success Spell:

- Select a yellow or orange candle to symbolize success and opportunity.
- Carve symbols or words related to your career goals onto the candle.
- Anoint the candle with a success-promoting oil, such as bergamot or ginger oil.
- Light the candle and visualize yourself excelling in your chosen career path.
- Focus on attracting recognition, promotions, and new opportunities.
- See yourself achieving your professional goals and experiencing career success.

o Let the candle burn down completely, affirming your commitment to your career success.

3. Business Prosperity Spell:

o Choose a green or purple candle, representing business growth and prosperity.

o Carve symbols or words related to your business goals onto the candle.

o Anoint the candle with an abundance-enhancing oil, such as basil or vetiver oil.

o Light the candle and visualize your business thriving and expanding.

o Focus on attracting new customers, financial abundance, and success in your business ventures.

o See your business becoming a magnet for prosperity and abundance.

o Allow the candle to burn for a specific period each day until it is extinguished, energizing your business endeavors.

4. Generosity and Gratitude Spell:

o Select a gold or yellow candle to symbolize gratitude and the flow of abundance.

o Carve symbols or words representing gratitude onto the candle.

o Anoint the candle with a gratitude-infused
  oil, such as citrus or rose oil.

o Light the candle and focus on feelings of
  gratitude for the abundance already present in your life.

o Visualize yourself sharing your abundance
  and practicing acts of generosity.

o See the flow of abundance expanding as
  you give and receive with an open heart.

o Let the candle burn down completely, expressing gratitude for the abundance that
  surrounds you.

When practicing prosperity and abundance spells,
it is important to cultivate a mindset of gratitude,
abundance, and ethical consideration. Align your intentions with the greater good, and be open to opportunities and avenues through which abundance can
manifest in your life.

Candle magic spells for prosperity and abundance
can help shift your mindset, attract positive financial
energy, and open doors to opportunities. Use them as
tools to support your financial goals, but also remember to cultivate a balanced approach to wealth and to
share your abundance with others.

# DIVINATION AND PSYCHIC ENHANCEMENT SPELLS

D ivination and psychic enhancement spells are an integral part of candle magic, allowing practitioners to access their intuitive abilities, gain insights, and connect with higher realms of consciousness. These spells utilize the power of intention, focused energy, and symbolism to enhance psychic awareness and facilitate divination practices. Here are some divination and psychic enhancement spells you can practice with candles:

1.  Third Eye Activation Spell:

    o   Choose a purple or indigo candle, symbolizing intuition and spiritual insight.
    o   Carve symbols or words representing the third eye onto the candle.

- Anoint the candle with a psychic-enhancing oil, such as mugwort or sandal-wood oil.
- Light the candle and visualize a radiant purple light emanating from your third eye.
- Focus on activating and opening your intuitive faculties.
- See yourself receiving clear psychic impressions and insights.
- Allow the candle to burn down completely, symbolizing the activation of your third eye.

2. Tarot or Oracle Card Enhancement Spell:

- Select a candle color that resonates with the energy of the cards you'll be working with.
- Carve symbols or words representing divination onto the candle.
- Anoint the candle with oil that enhances intuition and connection, such as jasmine or yarrow oil.
- Light the candle and hold your deck of cards in your hands.
- Focus on infusing the cards with your psychic energy and intention to receive accurate and insightful readings.

- See the candle's flame illuminating the hidden meanings within the cards.
- Let the candle burn for a specific period each time you perform a reading, creating a sacred space for divination.

3. Scrying and Crystal Gazing Spell:

- Choose a black or dark blue candle to represent the mystery and depth of scrying.
- Carve symbols or words related to scrying onto the candle.
- Anoint the candle with a psychic-enhancing oil, such as lavender or clary sage oil.
- Light the candle and set up your scrying or crystal gazing tool, such as a black mirror or crystal ball.
- Focus your gaze on the reflective surface, allowing your mind to enter a receptive state.
- See the candle's flame enhancing your psychic vision and facilitating deeper insights.
- Allow the candle to burn for the duration of your scrying session, maintaining a focused and receptive state.

4. Dream Enhancement Spell:

   o Select a blue or silver candle to represent the realm of dreams and the subconscious.
   o Carve symbols or words related to dreams onto the candle.
   o Anoint the candle with a dream-enhancing oil, such as lavender or mugwort oil.
   o Light the candle and place it on your nightstand or beside your bed.
   o Before sleep, focus your intention on vivid and insightful dreams.
   o See the candle's flame as a guiding light through the dream realm.
   o Allow the candle to burn out safely during the night, inviting enhanced dream recall and prophetic dreams.

When practicing divination and psychic enhancement spells, it is important to create a sacred space, center your energy, and approach the practice with respect and openness. Trust your intuitive guidance and honor the messages received during your divination practices.

Candle magic spells for divination and psychic enhancement serve as tools to deepen your intuitive connection, expand your psychic abilities, and gain profound insights. Use them in conjunction with your preferred divination methods, such as tarot, scrying, or dream interpretation, to enhance your spiritual practices.

# ELEMENTAL CANDLE SPELLS

E lemental candle spells harness the power of the four elements—earth, air, fire, and water—to create balance, invoke specific energies, and manifest desired outcomes. Each element represents different qualities and energies, and by incorporating them into your candle magic, you can amplify the intention and effectiveness of your spells. Here are some elemental candle spells you can practice:

1. Earth Element Spell:

   o Choose a green or brown candle, symbolizing the earth element and its grounding qualities.

   o Carve symbols or words related to stability, abundance, or growth onto the candle.

- Anoint the candle with a grounding oil, such as patchouli or vetiver oil.
- Light the candle and connect with the energy of the earth element.
- Focus on manifesting stability, grounding, and material abundance in your life.
- Visualize roots extending from the candle into the earth, anchoring your intentions.
- Let the candle burn down completely, symbolizing the solid foundation and growth of your desires.

2. Air Element Spell:

- Select a yellow or white candle to represent the air element and its qualities of communication and clarity.
- Carve symbols or words related to intellect, inspiration, or clear communication onto the candle.
- Anoint the candle with an uplifting oil, such as lemon or eucalyptus oil.
- Light the candle and connect with the energy of the air element.
- Focus on enhancing your communication skills, gaining mental clarity, or seeking inspiration.

- o Visualize the candle's flame carrying your intentions on the wings of the wind, spreading them far and wide.
- o Allow the candle to burn down completely, symbolizing the manifestation of clear communication or inspired ideas.

3. Fire Element Spell:

- o Choose a red or orange candle, symbolizing the fire element and its transformative and passionate energies.
- o Carve symbols or words related to energy, courage, or transformation onto the candle.
- o Anoint the candle with a fiery oil, such as cinnamon or ginger oil.
- o Light the candle and connect with the energy of the fire element.
- o Focus on igniting your passions, boosting your energy levels, or invoking transformation.
- o Visualize the candle's flame empowering and energizing your intentions, burning away obstacles.
- o Let the candle burn down completely, symbolizing the transformation and manifestation of your desires.

4. Water Element Spell:

  o Select a blue or silver candle to represent the water element and its emotional and intuitive qualities.

  o Carve symbols or words related to emotions, intuition, or healing onto the candle.

  o Anoint the candle with a water-enhancing oil, such as jasmine or lavender oil.

  o Light the candle and connect with the energy of the water element.

  o Focus on emotional healing, intuition, or enhancing your psychic abilities.

  o Visualize the candle's flame as a gentle flowing stream, cleansing and soothing your emotions.

  o Allow the candle to burn down completely, symbolizing emotional healing and the flow of intuitive insights.

When working with elemental candle spells, it is essential to honor and respect the energies of the elements. Use your intuition to guide you in selecting the appropriate colors, symbols, and oils that resonate with the specific elemental qualities you wish to invoke.

Elemental candle spells offer a powerful way to connect with the energies of the elements and manifest your intentions. Experiment with different elemental combinations and explore the unique qualities and correspondences of each element to enhance your candle magic practice.

# LUNAR AND SOLAR CANDLE MAGIC

L unar and solar candle magic draws upon the energies of the moon and the sun, harnessing their celestial influence to amplify intentions, manifest desires, and align with the cycles of nature. The moon represents the feminine, intuitive, and receptive energies, while the sun embodies the masculine, active, and radiant energies. By working with lunar and solar energies in your candle magic, you can tap into their unique qualities and synchronize your spells with the rhythms of the cosmos. Here are some lunar and solar candle magic techniques you can explore:

1. Lunar Candle Magic:

   o Choose a white or silver candle to symbolize the moon's energy and its connection to intuition, emotions, and feminine power.

73

- o Perform your candle magic rituals during specific lunar phases, such as the New Moon for new beginnings, the Full Moon for heightened energy, or the Waxing Moon for growth and expansion.
- o Carve symbols or words related to your intentions onto the candle.
- o Anoint the candle with a lunar-enhancing oil, such as jasmine or moonflower oil.
- o Light the candle and connect with the energy of the moon.
- o Focus on your intentions, visualizing them as the moon's light shining upon your desires.
- o Allow the candle to burn down completely or extinguish it when you feel your intention has been set.

2. Solar Candle Magic:

- o Select a gold or yellow candle to represent the sun's energy and its connection to vitality, abundance, and masculine power.
- o Perform your candle magic rituals during times of the day when the sun is strongest, such as sunrise or midday.

- Carve symbols or words related to your intentions onto the candle.
- Anoint the candle with a solar-enhancing oil, such as bergamot or frankincense oil.
- Light the candle and connect with the energy of the sun.
- Focus on your intentions, visualizing them as the sun's radiant energy infusing your desires with vitality and abundance.
- Allow the candle to burn down completely or extinguish it when you feel your intention has been empowered.

3. Lunar-Solar Balance Spell:

- Choose both a white or silver candle (for the moon) and a gold or yellow candle (for the sun).
- Carve symbols or words representing balance or harmony onto each candle.
- Anoint the moon candle with lunar-enhancing oil and the sun candle with solar-enhancing oil.
- Light both candles simultaneously, acknowledging the union of lunar and solar energies.

o   Focus on balancing and harmonizing your intentions, invoking both the receptive and active aspects of your desires.

o   See the candles' flames dancing together, merging the qualities of intuition and action.

o   Allow the candles to burn down completely or extinguish them when you feel the energies have aligned.

When working with lunar and solar candle magic, it is beneficial to tune in to the current lunar phase or the sun's position to align your intentions with the corresponding energies. You can also explore specific lunar and solar correspondences, such as using specific colors, crystals, or herbs that resonate with the moon or sun's energies.

Lunar and solar candle magic provides a powerful way to connect with celestial energies and synchronize your intentions with the natural cycles of the moon and sun. Experiment with different lunar phases, solar times, and correspondences to enhance your candle magic practice and deepen your connection to cosmic energies.

# ANCESTRAL CANDLE SPELLS

Ancestral candle spells are a profound way to honor and connect with your ancestors, seek their guidance, and receive their blessings. These spells provide a means to establish a spiritual connection with your lineage, tap into ancestral wisdom, and invoke the support and protection of your ancestors. Here are some ancestral candle spells you can practice:

1.  Ancestral Altar Candle Spell:

    o   Create a dedicated ancestral altar space, adorned with pictures, mementos, or symbols representing your ancestors.
    o   Place a white or ivory candle on the altar, symbolizing purity and connection with the ancestral realm.

- Light the candle, centering your energy and focusing on the intention to connect with your ancestors.
- Speak their names aloud or silently, acknowledging their presence and inviting their guidance and support.
- Share stories or memories, express gratitude, or seek guidance from your ancestors.
- Visualize the candle's flame as a bridge between the physical and spiritual realms, illuminating the path for ancestral connection.
- Allow the candle to burn for a specific period or until it extinguishes naturally, representing the time spent in communion with your ancestors.

2. Ancestral Guidance Candle Spell:

- Choose a purple or lavender candle, symbolizing spiritual connection and intuition.
- Carve symbols or words related to ancestral guidance onto the candle.
- Anoint the candle with oil that enhances spiritual connection, such as frankincense or myrrh oil.

- o Light the candle, focusing on the intention to receive guidance and wisdom from your ancestors.
- o Meditate or enter a receptive state, opening yourself to receive messages or insights from your ancestral spirits.
- o Trust your intuition and any signs, symbols, or sensations that arise during the candle spell.
- o Let the candle burn down completely or extinguish it when you feel your connection with your ancestors has been established.

3. Ancestral Healing Candle Spell:

- o Select a blue or green candle, symbolizing healing and emotional well-being.
- o Carve symbols or words related to ancestral healing onto the candle.
- o Anoint the candle with healing oil, such as lavender or rosemary oil.
- o Light the candle, focusing on the intention to heal ancestral wounds or patterns within your lineage.
- o Visualize the candle's flame as a transformative light, cleansing and healing ancestral energies.

- o Offer words of healing and forgiveness to your ancestors, acknowledging any pain or trauma that may be carried through generations.
- o Allow the candle to burn down completely, symbolizing the release and transformation of ancestral energies.

When practicing ancestral candle spells, it is important to approach the ritual with reverence, respect, and an open heart. Trust your intuition and the messages you receive from your ancestors, and remember to express gratitude for their presence and guidance.

Ancestral candle spells provide a powerful way to honor your lineage, establish a connection with your ancestors, and seek their guidance and blessings. As you deepen your relationship with your ancestral spirits, you may find increased support, healing, and a sense of belonging as you navigate your spiritual path.

# SABBAT AND ESBAT CANDLE RITUALS

S abbats and Esbats are important occasions in Wiccan practice that celebrate the cycles of the seasons and the moon. These rituals honor the natural rhythms of the Earth and the divine energy that permeates all of creation. Incorporating candle magic into Sabbat and Esbat rituals can deepen your connection with these sacred moments and enhance the energy you raise during these ceremonies. Here are some ideas for Sabbat and Esbat candle rituals:

1.  Sabbat Candle Ritual:

    o   Choose a candle color that corresponds to the specific Sabbat you are celebrating. For example, green for Ostara (Spring Equinox), red for Samhain (Halloween), or yellow for Litha (Summer Solstice).

o Set up your ritual space with appropriate symbols, decorations, and seasonal items.

o Light the candle at the beginning of the ritual, invoking the energy and significance of the Sabbat.

o Perform rituals, chants, or spells that align with the theme of the Sabbat, incorporating the energy of the lit candle.

o Focus on the intention of the Sabbat, whether it's renewal, harvest, or honoring the ancestors.

o Allow the candle to burn throughout the ritual, symbolizing the presence and energy of the Sabbat.

o Extinguish the candle at the end of the ritual, expressing gratitude for the blessings received.

2. Esbat Candle Ritual:

o Choose a white or silver candle to represent the moon's energy during an Esbat ritual.

o Set up your ritual space with lunar symbols, crystals, and other items associated with the moon.

- Light the candle, acknowledging the presence and power of the moon in your practice.
- Perform rituals, meditations, or divination practices that focus on lunar energy and intuition.
- Use the candle's flame to charge crystals, tools, or ritual objects with lunar energy.
- Reflect on your spiritual journey, set intentions, or seek guidance during the Esbat.
- Allow the candle to burn down completely or extinguish it at the end of the ritual, closing the sacred space.

Remember to personalize these rituals to align with your specific spiritual path and the traditions you follow. Consider incorporating chants, prayers, or invocations that resonate with your beliefs and intentions for the Sabbat or Esbat celebration.

Sabbat and Esbat candle rituals provide a beautiful opportunity to connect with the cycles of nature, honor the divine energy, and deepen your spiritual practice. By infusing candle magic into these rituals, you can amplify the energy and intention of these sacred moments, creating a deeper sense of connection and harmony with the natural and spiritual world around you.

# SELF-DISCOVERY AND PERSONAL GROWTH

Candle spells for self-discovery and personal growth are a powerful way to embark on a journey of self-reflection, inner exploration, and transformation. These spells can help you uncover your true essence, release limiting beliefs, and cultivate positive qualities within yourself. Here are some candle spells for self-discovery and personal growth:

1. Mirror Reflection Spell:

   o Sit in a quiet and comfortable space with a mirror placed in front of you.
   o Choose a white candle to represent clarity and self-reflection.
   o Light the candle, gaze into the mirror, and focus on your reflection.

- Repeat affirmations or statements that affirm your desire for self-discovery and personal growth.
- Allow any emotions, insights, or revelations to surface as you gaze at your reflection.
- Journal or meditate on the thoughts and feelings that arise, exploring your inner landscape.
- Blow out the candle, expressing gratitude for the insights gained and your commitment to personal growth.

2. Release and Renewal Spell:

- Select a black candle to symbolize the release of old patterns or beliefs.
- Light the candle, holding it in your hands, and visualize the aspects of yourself or limiting beliefs you wish to let go of.
- Speak out loud or silently affirmations that reflect your intention to release and transform.
- Envision the candle's flame burning away the old patterns, freeing you to embrace new possibilities.

- Place the candle in a fire-safe container and let it burn down completely, symbolizing the release and renewal process.
- Dispose of the candle remnants, recognizing that you have made space for personal growth and positive change.

3. Empowerment Spell:

- Choose a yellow or orange candle to represent empowerment and self-confidence.
- Light the candle, hold it in your hands, and visualize yourself embodying the qualities you wish to cultivate.
- Recite affirmations or mantras that affirm your inner strength, worthiness, and personal growth.
- Allow the candle's flame to infuse you with its empowering energy, boosting your confidence and self-belief.
- Take inspired action toward your personal growth goals, trusting in your abilities.
- Let the candle burn down completely, symbolizing the integration of your empowered self.

4. Intuition and Inner Wisdom Spell:

- Select a purple or indigo candle to symbolize intuition and inner wisdom.
- Light the candle, sit in a meditative posture, and focus on your breath to center yourself.
- Ask for guidance and insights from your intuition and inner wisdom.
- Pay attention to any thoughts, feelings, or sensations that arise during the candle spell.
- Trust your inner knowing and allow your intuition to guide you in your personal growth journey.
- Journal or reflect on the messages or guidance you received, noting how you can apply them to your life.
- Extinguish the candle, expressing gratitude for the wisdom and guidance received.

Remember to approach these self-discovery and personal growth candle spells with an open heart and a willingness to explore the depths of your being. Embrace the insights, challenges, and growth that come your way as you embark on this transformative journey of self-discovery.

# CLEARING NEGATIVE ENERGY AND CURSES

C andle spells for clearing negative energy and curses can help you cleanse your energetic space, release stagnant or harmful vibrations, and restore harmony and positivity in your life. These spells are designed to remove any negative influences or obstacles that may be affecting your wellbeing. Here are some candle spells for clearing negative energy and curses:

1.  Purification Candle Spell:

    o Select a white or lavender candle to symbolize purification and cleansing.
    o Create a sacred space by clearing clutter and setting an intention for energetic purification.

- Light the candle, focusing on its flame as a purifying force that transforms negative energy into light.
- Visualize the candle's flame enveloping you and your surroundings, cleansing and purifying the space.
- Speak or chant affirmations that declare your intention to release negative energy and invite positive vibrations.
- Allow the candle to burn down completely, symbolizing the complete purification of your space.

2. Uncrossing Candle Spell:

- Choose a black candle to symbolize the absorption and removal of negative energy.
- Carve symbols or words representing your desire to break curses or remove negative influences onto the candle.
- Light the candle, visualizing its flame as a powerful tool that breaks through any negative energy or curses.
- Call upon your spiritual guides or deities for assistance in removing negative influences.

o Speak or affirm statements that declare your intention to break free from any curses or negative energy.

o Allow the candle to burn down completely, visualizing the negative energy being absorbed and transmuted by the flame.

3. Protection Candle Spell:

o Select a white or blue candle to symbolize protection and shielding.

o Anoint the candle with protective oils such as frankincense, myrrh, or rosemary oil.

o Light the candle, visualizing its flame forming a protective barrier around you and your space.

o Repeat protective affirmations or prayers that invoke divine protection.

o Visualize the candle's flame as a source of divine light and energy that repels any negative influences or curses.

o Allow the candle to burn down completely, envisioning the protective energy surrounding you and your environment.

4. Banishing Candle Spell:

- Choose a black or red candle to represent banishing and releasing negative energy.
- Write down specific negative energies, curses, or influences you wish to banish on a piece of paper.
- Place the paper under the candle or attach it to the candle using a non-flammable holder.
- Light the candle, focusing on the flame as it burns away the negative energy and curses.
- Speak or chant incantations that affirm your intention to banish and release the negative influences.
- Allow the candle to burn down completely, visualizing the negative energies dissipating and being replaced by positive vibrations.

Remember to always work with intention, focus, and respect when performing candle spells for clearing negative energy and curses. Trust your intuition and adapt these spells to align with your specific situation and spiritual beliefs. As you release and clear away negative energy, you create space for positive and harmonious vibrations to enter your life.

# CAREER AND SUCCESS ENHANCEMENT

Candle spells for career and success enhancement can help you attract opportunities, boost your confidence, and manifest your professional goals. These spells are designed to align your energy with your desired career path, enhance your skills and abilities, and attract success and abundance. Here are some candle spells for career and success enhancement:

1. Success and Abundance Candle Spell:

   o Choose a green or gold candle to symbolize success and abundance.
   o Carve symbols or words representing your career goals onto the candle.
   o Anoint the candle with a success-enhancing oil such as cinnamon or bergamot oil.

- Light the candle, focus on the flame, and visualize yourself achieving your desired career success.
- Repeat affirmations or mantras that affirm your belief in your abilities and attract abundance.
- Meditate on the feelings of success, abundance, and fulfillment in your chosen career.
- Allow the candle to burn down completely, symbolizing the manifestation of career success and abundance.

2. Confidence and Empowerment Candle Spell:

- Select a yellow or orange candle to symbolize confidence and empowerment.
- Carve symbols or words representing confidence onto the candle.
- Anoint the candle with a confidence-boosting oil such as ginger or cedarwood oil.
- Light the candle, hold it in your hands, and visualize the flame infusing you with confidence and empowerment.

o Repeat affirmations or statements that affirm your belief in your skills, talents, and capabilities.

o Take inspired action towards your career goals, trusting in your abilities.

o Allow the candle to burn down completely or extinguish it at the end of the ritual, carrying the energy of confidence and empowerment with you.

3. Career Path Visualization Spell:

o Choose a blue or purple candle to symbolize clarity and intuition.

o Sit in a quiet and comfortable space, holding the candle in your hands.

o Close your eyes and take several deep breaths to center yourself.

o Visualize yourself in your desired career, engaged in fulfilling work, and achieving success.

o Envision the steps you need to take to manifest your career goals, seeing yourself overcoming challenges and achieving milestones.

o Speak or affirm statements that affirm your alignment with your desired career path.

- Open your eyes and light the candle, allowing its flame to represent the clarity and guidance on your career journey.
- Spend a few moments meditating on the visualization and expressing gratitude for the opportunities and success that will come your way.
- Let the candle burn down completely, carrying the energy of your career visualization into the universe.

4. Networking and Opportunity Attraction Spell:

- Select a pink or red candle to symbolize connection and attraction.
- Carve symbols or words representing networking and opportunities onto the candle.
- Anoint the candle with an attraction-enhancing oil such as patchouli or rose oil.
- Light the candle, envisioning its flame as a magnet that draws favorable connections and opportunities to you.
- Repeat affirmations or mantras that affirm your ability to network effectively and attract beneficial opportunities.

- o Take proactive steps to expand your professional network, such as attending events or reaching out to potential contacts.
- o Allow the candle to burn down completely, symbolizing the attraction of networking and opportunities in your career.

Remember to approach these career and success enhancement candle spells with a focused mindset, a clear intention, and a belief in your own abilities. Align your actions with your intentions, and trust that the universe will support you in manifesting your professional goals. As you infuse your energy with career-enhancing intentions, you pave the way for success, abundance, and fulfillment in your chosen career path.

# FERTILITY AND FAMILY BLESSINGS

C andle spells for fertility and family blessings can be used to enhance fertility, support healthy pregnancies, and foster a loving and harmonious family environment. These spells can help you connect with the energies of fertility and invoke blessings for conception, pregnancy, childbirth, and the well-being of your family. Here are some candle spells for fertility and family blessings:

1. Fertility Blessing Candle Spell:

    o Choose a green or yellow candle to symbolize fertility and growth.
    o Anoint the candle with a fertility-enhancing oil such as jasmine or geranium oil.
    o Light the candle, focusing on its flame and visualizing yourself and your partner in a state of fertile energy.

- o Offer prayers or blessings to deities associated with fertility, such as the goddesses Aphrodite or Freya.
- o Speak or affirm statements that declare your intention to conceive and nurture new life.
- o Visualize your body as a fertile ground, ready to receive the gift of new life.
- o Allow the candle to burn down completely, symbolizing the manifestation of fertility and the creation of new life.

2. Pregnancy Protection Candle Spell:

- o Select a blue or white candle to symbolize protection and purity.
- o Anoint the candle with a protective oil such as lavender or frankincense oil.
- o Light the candle, holding it in your hands, and visualize a protective light surrounding you and your unborn child.
- o Offer prayers or invocations to deities associated with motherhood and protection, such as the goddess Artemis or Mother Mary.

- Repeat affirmations or mantras that affirm the health, well-being, and protection of your pregnancy.
- Envision your unborn child surrounded by love, safety, and nurturing energy.
- Allow the candle to burn down completely or extinguish it at the end of the ritual, carrying the energy of protection throughout your pregnancy.

3. Blessing the Home and Family Candle Spell:

- Choose a white or pink candle to symbolize purity and love.
- Carve symbols or words representing love, harmony, and blessings onto the candle.
- Light the candle in the heart of your home, such as the living room or family altar.
- Speak or chant blessings and prayers for the well-being and happiness of your family.
- Visualize your home filled with love, joy, and positive energy, nurturing and supporting each family member.
- Offer gratitude for the blessings and experiences that your family shares.

o Allow the candle to burn down completely, infusing your home with the energy of love and family blessings.

4. Family Unity and Healing Candle Spell:

o Select a purple or white candle to symbolize spiritual healing and unity.

o Anoint the candle with a healing oil such as eucalyptus or rosemary oil.

o Light the candle, inviting all family members to gather around it.

o Hold hands and create a circle of unity, expressing love and forgiveness for each other.

o Share heartfelt affirmations or blessings, expressing your desire for unity and healing within the family.

o Visualize any past conflicts or challenges dissolving and transforming into love and understanding.

o Allow the candle to burn down completely, symbolizing the healing and unity of your family.

Approach these fertility and family blessing candle spells with love, openness, and a deep connection to the energies of fertility and family. Trust in the power of your intentions and the divine support that surrounds you as you invoke blessings for conception, pregnancy, and the well-being of your family. Embrace the journey of fertility and family life with gratitude and joy, knowing that you are supported by the loving energies of the universe.

# SPIRIT COMMUNICATION AND DREAM WORK

Candle spells for spirit communication and dream work can help you deepen your connection with the spiritual realm, enhance your psychic abilities, and receive guidance and messages from the unseen realms. These spells can assist you in developing a stronger connection with your intuition, accessing higher wisdom, and exploring the realm of dreams. Here are some candle spells for spirit communication and dream work:

1.  Spirit Communication Candle Spell:

    o   Choose a purple or indigo candle to symbolize spiritual connection and intuition.
    o   Anoint the candle with a psychic-enhancing oil such as sandalwood or mugwort oil.

- Light the candle, creating a quiet and sacred space for spirit communication.
- Focus your attention on the candle's flame, allowing it to become a focal point for your intention.
- Speak or silently invoke the presence of your spirit guides, ancestors, or departed loved ones.
- Open yourself to receive any messages, insights, or guidance from the spiritual realm.
- Trust your intuition and be open to signs, symbols, or sensations that may indicate spiritual communication.
- Allow the candle to burn down completely, expressing gratitude for the connection with the spiritual realm.

2. Dream Enhancement Candle Spell:

- Select a blue or silver candle to symbolize dreams, intuition, and psychic abilities.
- Anoint the candle with a dream-enhancing oil such as lavender or chamomile oil.
- Light the candle, creating a peaceful and serene atmosphere in your sleeping area.

- Set your intention to enhance your dream recall and invite insightful and meaningful dreams.
- Keep a dream journal nearby to record your dreams upon waking.
- Before sleeping, focus on the candle's flame, visualizing it as a gateway to the realm of dreams.
- Repeat affirmations or mantras that affirm your desire for vivid, enlightening, and spiritually significant dreams.
- Upon waking, take a moment to record your dreams in your journal, reflecting on any symbols, messages, or insights they may hold.
- Allow the candle to burn down completely or extinguish it at the end of the ritual, carrying the energy of dream enhancement with you.

3. Ancestor Communication Candle Spell:

- Choose a white or black candle to symbolize a connection with your ancestors.
- Carve symbols or words representing your ancestral lineage onto the candle.

- Anoint the candle with an ancestor-connecting oil such as cedarwood or rosemary oil.
- Light the candle, creating a quiet and reverent space for ancestor communication.
- Speak or silently call upon your ancestors, inviting their presence and guidance.
- Share stories, memories, or thoughts about your ancestors, expressing your desire to connect with them.
- Trust your intuition and be open to any signs, synchronicities, or messages that may come through during the ritual.
- Allow the candle to burn down completely, expressing gratitude for the wisdom and support of your ancestors.

Approach these spirit communication and dreamwork candle spells with reverence, openness, and a willingness to receive messages and insights from the spiritual realm. Create a sacred space and set clear intentions before engaging in these practices. Trust in the divine guidance and wisdom that is available to you as you deepen your connection with the spiritual realm and explore the realm of dreams.

# FULL MOON
# CANDLE RITUAL

The full moon is a potent time for manifestation, release, and deepening your spiritual connection. This candle ritual harnesses the energy of the full moon to amplify your intentions and align your energy with the lunar cycles. Here is a step-by-step guide for a full moon candle ritual:

Materials Needed:

- White or silver candle
- Candle holder
- Matches or lighter
- Journal or paper
- Pen or pencil

Instructions:

1. Preparation:

- Choose a quiet and undisturbed space where you can perform the ritual.
- Set up your materials, placing the candle in its holder in front of you.
- Light some incense or use a smudge stick to cleanse the space and create a sacred atmosphere.
- Take a few deep breaths to center yourself and quiet your mind.

2. Setting Intentions:

- Hold the candle in your hands and close your eyes.
- Reflect on your intentions for the upcoming lunar cycle and the areas of your life you wish to focus on.
- Visualize these intentions as already manifested, feeling the emotions associated with their fulfillment.
- When you are ready, speak your intentions aloud or silently in your mind, stating them clearly and with conviction.

3. Lighting the Candle:

- Light the candle with a match or lighter, as you focus on the flame.

- As you do so, say a simple affirmation or invocation to activate the energy of the full moon.
- Example: "I light this candle to align my energy with the powerful energy of the full moon. May its light illuminate my path and manifest my intentions."

4. Writing in Your Journal:

- Take your journal or a piece of paper and write down your intentions in detail.
- Express your desires, goals, and aspirations, focusing on the positive outcomes you wish to manifest.
- Use descriptive language and affirmations that resonate with you.
- Take your time to reflect on each intention and infuse it with your energy and intention.

5. Candle Visualization:

- Hold your written intentions in one hand and gaze at the flame of the candle.
- Visualize the energy of the full moon pouring into the candle, infusing it with power and amplifying your intentions.

- Imagine the light of the candle expanding and radiating your intentions out into the universe.
- See your desires and goals being supported and brought into manifestation.

6. Affirmations and Gratitude:

- Read your intentions aloud, affirming them with conviction and gratitude.
- Express gratitude for the blessings already present in your life and for the fulfillment of your intentions.
- Feel a sense of appreciation and trust that the universe is working in your favor.

7. Closing the Ritual:

- Once you have finished reading your intentions and expressing gratitude, extinguish the candle safely.
- Place your written intentions in a sacred space, such as an altar, or keep them in your journal as a reminder.
- Take a moment to ground yourself by taking deep breaths and feeling your connection to the earth beneath you.

Remember to repeat this ritual during each full moon to continuously align your energy with the lunar cycles and amplify your intentions. You can adapt and personalize the ritual based on your own beliefs and preferences. Embrace the power of the full moon and trust in the manifestation of your intentions as you work with the energy of the lunar cycle.

# NEW MOON
# CANDLE RITUAL

The new moon is a potent time for setting new intentions, planting seeds of growth, and embarking on new beginnings. This candle ritual harnesses the energy of the new moon to support you in manifesting your desires and welcoming positive change into your life. Here is a step-by-step guide for a new moon candle ritual:

Materials Needed:

- Black or dark blue candle
- Candle holder
- Matches or lighter
- Journal or paper
- Pen or pencil

Instructions:

1. Preparation:

   o   Find a quiet and comfortable space where you can perform the ritual without interruptions.

   o   Set up your materials, placing the candle in its holder in front of you.

   o   Light some incense or use a smudge stick to cleanse the space and create a sacred atmosphere.

   o   Take a few moments to ground yourself by taking deep breaths and centering your energy.

2. Setting Intentions:

   o   Hold the candle in your hands and close your eyes.

   o   Reflect on your desires, goals, and areas of your life that you wish to bring new energy and positive change to.

   o   Visualize these intentions as already fulfilled, feeling the excitement and joy associated with their manifestation.

- When you are ready, speak your intentions aloud or silently in your mind, stating them clearly and with conviction.

3. Lighting the Candle:

- Light the candle with a match or lighter, focusing your attention on the flame.
- As you do so, say a simple affirmation or invocation to activate the energy of the new moon.
- Example: "I light this candle to align my energy with the transformative energy of the new moon. May its light guide me in manifesting my intentions and embracing new beginnings."

4. Writing in Your Journal:

- Take your journal or a piece of paper and write down your intentions in detail.
- Be specific and clear about what you wish to manifest during this new moon cycle.
- Use positive language and affirmations that resonate with you.
- Take your time to reflect on each intention, infusing it with your energy and intention.

113

5. Candle Visualization:

- ○ Hold your written intentions in one hand and gaze at the flame of the candle.
- ○ Visualize the energy of the new moon infusing the candle, empowering your intentions and igniting new possibilities.
- ○ Imagine the flame representing the transformative energy of the new moon, illuminating your path and guiding you towards your desires.
- ○ See your intentions taking shape and manifesting with every breath you take.

6. Affirmations and Gratitude:

- ○ Read your intentions aloud, affirming them with confidence and gratitude.
- ○ Express gratitude for the opportunities and new beginnings that are coming your way.
- ○ Feel a deep sense of appreciation and trust in the universe's support of your journey.

7. Closing the Ritual:

- ○ Once you have finished reading your intentions and expressing gratitude, extinguish the candle safely.

- Place your written intentions in a sacred space, such as an altar, or keep them in your journal as a reminder.
- Take a moment to ground yourself by placing your hands on the ground, feeling your connection to the earth beneath you.

Remember to repeat this ritual during each new moon to set new intentions, align your energy with the lunar cycle, and invite positive change into your life. Feel free to customize the ritual to suit your personal beliefs and preferences. Embrace the energy of the new moon and trust in the manifestation of your intentions as you embark on new beginnings and invite growth and transformation into your life.

# SEASONAL CANDLE CELEBRATIONS

C andle rituals can be enhanced by incorporating the energy and symbolism of the changing seasons. By aligning your candle magic with the cycles of nature, you can deepen your connection to the Earth and harness the unique energies present during each season. Here are some ideas for seasonal candle celebrations:

1. Spring Equinox Candle Ritual:

   o Use pastel-colored candles to represent the vibrant energy of spring.
   o Light candles in honor of new beginnings, growth, and fertility.
   o Set intentions for personal growth, renewal, and manifesting new opportunities.

- Reflect on the balance between light and darkness as the days grow longer.
- Incorporate symbols of rebirth and transformation, such as flowers or bird feathers.

2. Summer Solstice Candle Ritual:

- Choose candles in fiery colors like red, orange, and gold to symbolize the warmth and energy of summer.
- Light candles to celebrate the peak of abundance and the power of the sun.
- Set intentions for creativity, passion, and fulfillment.
- Reflect on the abundance in your life and express gratitude for the blessings received.
- Incorporate symbols of the sun, such as sunflowers or sun-themed decorations.

3. Autumn Equinox Candle Ritual:

- Select candles in rich, earthy tones like brown, orange, and deep red to represent the colors of autumn.
- Light candles to honor the harvest, gratitude, and balance between light and darkness.

- o Set intentions for grounding, releasing what no longer serves you, and embracing change.
- o Reflect on the cycles of life, death, and transformation present in nature.
- o Incorporate symbols of the harvest, such as fruits, vegetables, or fallen leaves.

4. Winter Solstice Candle Ritual:

- o Use candles in cool, wintry colors like white, silver, and blue to evoke the stillness and magic of winter.
- o Light candles to celebrate the return of light and the rebirth of the sun.
- o Set intentions for inner reflection, healing, and finding light in the darkness.
- o Reflect on the power of patience, rest, and introspection during the winter season.
- o Incorporate symbols of the winter solstice, such as evergreen branches or snowflakes.

5. Seasonal Transition Candle Rituals:

- o At the turning points between seasons, you can create candle rituals to honor the energy of transition.

- Use candles that represent the departing season and candles that symbolize the upcoming season.
- Reflect on the lessons learned and experiences gained during the previous season.
- Set intentions for embracing the new season and welcoming its unique energy and opportunities.
- Incorporate symbols that bridge the gap between the seasons, such as seashells for the transition from summer to autumn or blooming flowers for the transition from winter to spring.

Remember to create a sacred space, set clear intentions, and infuse your candle rituals with personal meaning and symbolism. You can adapt these suggestions to suit your own spiritual path and connection with the seasons. By honoring the cycles of nature through candle celebrations, you deepen your connection to the Earth and align your energy with the natural rhythms of life.

# HANDFASTING AND WEDDING CANDLE CEREMONIES

Handfasting and wedding ceremonies are beautiful occasions to celebrate love, commitment, and the joining of two individuals. Candle ceremonies can be incorporated into these special events to add an extra layer of symbolism and ritual. Here is a guide for conducting handfasting and wedding candle ceremonies:

1. Preparation:

   o Set up a central altar or table where the ceremony will take place.

   o Place two taper candles, representing each partner, on either side of a larger unity candle or a central pillar candle.

- Decorate the altar with flowers, symbols of love and unity, and any other meaningful items.

2. Opening Blessing:

- Begin the ceremony with an opening blessing or invocation, setting the sacred tone of the occasion.
- Invite any deities, ancestors, or spiritual guides that you wish to be present during the ceremony.

3. Lighting the Individual Candles:

- Each partner takes their respective taper candle.
- Together, they light their individual candles, symbolizing their individuality and unique qualities.
- As they light the candles, they can express words of love, commitment, and gratitude to each other.

4. Handfasting Ritual:

- The couple's hands are joined together, symbolizing their union and the binding of their love.

- o A ribbon or cord is wrapped around their joined hands, forming the handfasting knot.
- o Words of commitment, vows, or promises are spoken during this moment.

5. Lighting the Unity Candle:

- o The couple takes their joined hands and together lights the unity candle or central pillar candle.
- o This act represents the merging of their lives and the creation of a unified partnership.
- o As they light the unity candle, they can express their hopes, dreams, and intentions for their shared future.

6. Exchange of Rings:

- o If rings are being exchanged, this is an opportune time to do so.
- o The rings can be blessed or charged with intentions for lifelong commitment and love.

7. Closing Blessing:

- o Conclude the ceremony with a closing blessing, expressing gratitude for love, union, and the sacredness of the occasion.

- Offer words of blessing for the couple's journey together and their shared future.

8. Extinguishing the Individual Candles:

- The couple can each take turns extinguishing their individual taper candles.
- This act symbolizes leaving behind their individual lives to embrace their united path.

9. Unity Candle Keepsake:

- The unity candle or central pillar candle can be kept as a special keepsake, a reminder of the ceremony and the love shared.

Remember to personalize the ceremony to reflect the beliefs, values, and preferences of the couple. Incorporate readings, prayers, or rituals that hold significance for you and your partner. The candle ceremony serves as a visual representation of the love, unity, and commitment being celebrated, creating a memorable and heartfelt experience for all involved.

# INTENTION SETTING AND SPELL DESIGN

I ntention setting and spell design are fundamental aspects of candle magic in Wicca. By clearly defining your intentions and crafting spells that align with your desires, you can effectively harness the energy of candle magic to manifest your goals. Here is a guide to help you with intention setting and spell design:

1. Reflect on Your Intentions:

   o Take time to explore and clarify your intentions. What is it that you truly desire to manifest or change in your life? Be specific and clear about your goals.

   o Consider the ethical implications of your intentions and ensure that they align with the Wiccan Rede, promoting harmlessness and positive growth.

2. Choose the Right Candle:

- Select a candle that corresponds to your intention based on color symbolism. Refer to the color correspondences section in your book to understand the meanings associated with different candle colors.
- You can also consider adding herbs, oils, or inscriptions on the candle that further enhance its alignment with your intention.

3. Craft Your Spell:

- Write down your spell in a clear and concise manner. Start with a statement of intention, affirming what you wish to manifest.
- Include any specific actions, words, or rituals that are essential to your spell. This can be as simple or elaborate as you desire.
- Incorporate elements of visualization, affirmation, and focused intent into your spell. Visualize your desired outcome as already achieved and infuse your words with belief and conviction.

4. Timing Considerations:

- Consider the timing of your spell to enhance its effectiveness. Refer to the section on timing and astrological considerations in your book to understand the significance of different lunar phases, days of the week, or planetary influences.

o  Choose a timing that aligns with the energy and symbolism associated with your intention.

5.  Ritual Preparation:

o  Create a sacred space for your ritual. Cleanse the area, light incense, and set up any additional tools or items that you feel are appropriate.

o  Ground yourself through meditation, deep breathing, or other grounding techniques. Center your energy and focus on your intention.

6.  Perform the Spell:

o  Light the candle, dedicating it to your intention. You can recite a simple incantation or invocation that affirms your purpose.

o  Focus your attention on the flame of the candle, visualizing your intention manifesting with clarity and purpose.

- Speak or recite your spell, infusing each word with intention and energy. Feel the power of your words and the energy of the candle merging together.

7. Closing the Ritual:

- Express gratitude for the energy and assistance received during the spellwork.
- Safely extinguish the candle, either by blowing it out or snuffing it with a candle snuffer.
- Ground yourself once again, releasing any excess energy and returning to a balanced state.

Remember that intention setting and spell design are deeply personal processes. Adapt and modify the guidelines provided to suit your own beliefs, preferences, and intuitive guidance. With practice, you will become more attuned to the energy of candle magic and better able to design spells that effectively manifest your intentions.

# INCORPORATING HERBS, OILS, AND SYMBOLS

Incorporating herbs, oils, and symbols into your candle magic can enhance the energy and intention of your spells. These additional elements carry their own correspondences and properties, adding depth and potency to your practice. Here's a guide to help you incorporate herbs, oils, and symbols into your candle magic:

1. Herbs:

   o Choose herbs that align with your intention. Each herb has its own energetic properties and associations. Refer to a reputable herbal correspondence guide or your book for information on different herbs and their meanings.

- Prepare the herbs by drying and crushing them, or you can use pre-dried herbs available from reputable sources.
- Sprinkle the herbs around the base of the candle or roll the candle in the herbs, coating it with their energy.
- Alternatively, you can create herb-infused oils by steeping the herbs in a carrier oil, such as olive oil or jojoba oil. Use these oils to anoint the candle or draw symbols on it.

2. Oils:

- Essential oils are concentrated plant extracts that carry the energetic properties of the plants from which they are derived. Choose oils that resonate with your intention.
- Anoint the candle by applying a few drops of the chosen essential oil to your fingertips, then rub the oil onto the candle. Focus on your intention as you do this, infusing the oil with your desired outcome.
- You can also create your own oil blends by combining different essential oils that align with your specific intention. Experiment

and trust your intuition to create blends that resonate with you.

3. Symbols:

o  Symbols carry their own meanings and can be used to amplify your intention. Consider incorporating symbols that resonate with your desired outcome.

o  Draw or carve symbols onto the candle using a sharp object, such as a pin or a small knife. Some commonly used symbols in Wicca include pentagrams, spirals, hearts, runes, or personal sigils.

o  Visualize the symbol as you create it, infusing it with your intention and energy.

o  You can also place small symbols or charms around the candle, such as crystals, feathers, or seashells, that represent your intention.

4. Correspondences:

o  When incorporating herbs, oils, and symbols, consider their correspondences and align them with your intention and the desired outcome.

- Refer to your book or reliable sources for information on the correspondences of different herbs, oils, and symbols. Take note of their elemental associations, planetary influences, or energetic properties.
- Use this knowledge to select and combine herbs, oils, and symbols that harmonize with your intention and create a cohesive and powerful spell.

Remember to be mindful of ethical considerations and use herbs, oils, and symbols responsibly. Use organic and sustainably sourced materials whenever possible. Trust your intuition when choosing and combining these elements, as your own personal connection and resonance with them are essential. As you continue to explore and experiment, you will discover the unique combinations that work best for you and amplify the energy of your candle magic.

# PERSONALIZING CANDLE SPELLS

Personalizing your candle spells is an important aspect of connecting with the energy of the spell and making it uniquely yours. By infusing your own intentions, beliefs, and personal symbolism into your candle magic, you can create a deeper and more meaningful experience. Here are some ways to personalize your candle spells:

1. Intentions and Desires:

    o Take the time to reflect on your personal intentions and desires. What specific outcomes or changes do you seek in your life? Clarify your intentions and be specific about what you want to manifest.

    o Consider your personal values and beliefs. Ensure that your intentions align with your ethical and spiritual principles.

2. Words and Affirmations:

o Write your own words and affirmations for your candle spells. Personalize them to reflect your intentions and emotions. Speak from your heart and infuse your words with genuine emotion and conviction.

o Use positive language and present tense, as if your desired outcome has already manifested. This helps to create a sense of empowerment and belief in the spell.

3. Symbols and Imagery:

o Incorporate symbols and imagery that hold personal significance for you. Choose symbols that resonate with your intentions and connect with your intuition.

o Create your own symbols or sigils that represent your desires. Draw or carve them onto the candle, infusing them with your energy and intention.

o Visualize the symbols and imagery as you perform the spell, allowing them to amplify and empower your intention.

4. Personal Belief Systems:

o Draw upon your personal belief systems to enhance your candle spells. If you follow a specific spiritual path or tradition, incorporate elements from it into your spells.

o Adapt rituals, prayers, or invocations to align with your personal beliefs. Make the spell a reflection of your unique spiritual journey.

5. Timing and Astrological Influences:

o Consider how timing and astrological influences align with your personal energy and intentions. While there are general correspondences, trust your own intuition and awareness of your energetic cycles.

o Take note of the times of day, phases of the moon, or planetary aspects that resonate with you and incorporate them into your candle spells.

6. Emotional Connection:

o Connect with your emotions during the spellcasting process. Allow yourself to feel the emotions associated with your intentions, whether it's excitement, joy, gratitude, or determination.

- Infuse your candle with your emotions by holding it in your hands and visualizing your emotions flowing into the candle.

7. Intuitive Guidance:

- Trust your intuition and inner guidance when personalizing your candle spells. You have a unique connection to your desires and intentions, and your intuition can guide you in making the right choices for your spell.

Remember that personalization is about aligning with your authentic self and creating a meaningful connection with your candle spells. As you continue to practice and explore, you will discover your own personal touches and techniques that enhance the potency and effectiveness of your spells. Embrace your individuality and infuse your magic with your personal energy and intention.

# MANIFESTATION TECHNIQUES AND VISUALIZATION

Manifestation is a key aspect of candle magic in Wicca. By engaging in focused visualization techniques, you can harness the power of your mind and energy to bring your intentions to life. Here are some manifestation techniques and visualization practices to enhance your candle spells:

1. Setting Clear Intentions:

    o Before you begin your candle spell, take a moment to clarify your intentions. Clearly define what you want to manifest and be specific about the outcome you desire.

    o Write down your intentions on a piece of paper or in a journal. This helps to solidify your intentions and serves as a reminder during the manifestation process.

2. Visualization:

○ Visualization is a powerful technique that helps you create a mental image of your desired outcome. Close your eyes and imagine your intention as if it has already manifested.

○ Visualize the details of your desired outcome. Engage all your senses — see, hear, touch, smell, and even taste the experience of your intention coming to fruition.

○ Make your visualization as vivid and detailed as possible. Feel the emotions associated with your manifestation and allow yourself to fully immerse in the experience.

3. Affirmations and Positive Language:

○ Incorporate affirmations and positive language into your manifestation practice. Repeat empowering statements that affirm your belief in the manifestation of your intentions.

o   Use present tense language to create a sense of already having achieved your desired outcome. For example, say, "I am abundant and prosperous" rather than "I will be abundant and prosperous."

4.  Energy Alignment:

o   Align your energy with the vibration of your desired outcome. Imagine your energy field expanding and resonating with the energy of your intention.

o   Use your breath to amplify your energy. Inhale deeply, visualize yourself drawing in the energy of manifestation, and exhale, releasing any doubts or resistance.

o   Feel a sense of gratitude for the manifestation of your intention, as if it has already come to pass. This helps to raise your vibration and attract the desired outcome.

5.  Meditative State:

o   Enter a meditative state before and during your candle spell. Quiet your mind, release distractions, and focus your attention on your intention and visualization.

- o You can use meditation techniques such as deep breathing, progressive muscle relaxation, or guided visualizations to enter a state of heightened focus and receptivity.

6. Time and Consistency:

- o Consistency is key in manifestation. Set aside regular time for your candle spells and visualization practices.
- o Practice visualization and affirmation techniques daily, even outside of your candle spells. This helps to reinforce your intentions and create a consistent energy flow toward your desired outcome.

Remember that manifestation is a co-creative process between you, the Universe, and the energy you are working with. Trust in the power of your intentions, engage all your senses in the visualization process and maintain a positive and open mindset. By consistently practicing these manifestation techniques, you can amplify the effectiveness of your candle spells and bring your intentions to life.

# HARM NONE: THE WICCAN REDE

The Wiccan Rede is a guiding ethical principle in Wicca that emphasizes the importance of acting in ways that do not cause harm to others or oneself. It serves as a moral compass for Wiccans and encourages the practice of responsible and mindful actions. Here is an exploration of the Wiccan Rede and its significance in candle magic:

1.  Understanding the Wiccan Rede:

    o   The Wiccan Rede is often summarized by the phrase "An it harm none, do what ye will." This means that as long as your actions do not cause harm, you have the freedom to follow your own path and make choices in alignment with your true will.

o It promotes the idea of personal responsibility and the recognition of the interconnectedness of all beings. Wiccans strive to live in harmony with nature, others, and themselves.

2. Applying the Wiccan Rede to Candle Magic:

o In candle magic, the Wiccan Rede reminds practitioners to consider the potential consequences and ethical implications of their spellwork.

o Before casting a spell, reflect on its intention and the potential impact it may have on others. Ensure that it aligns with the principles of harm none and promotes positive and constructive outcomes.

o Avoid using candle magic to manipulate or control others, as this violates the spirit of the Rede. Instead, focus on empowering and supporting others in their own personal growth and well-being.

3. Ethical Considerations in Candle Magic:

o When working with candle spells, it is important to consider the ethics of your actions and their potential effects.

- o Obtain consent before performing candle magic on behalf of others. Respect their autonomy and allow them the freedom to make their own choices.
- o Avoid casting spells that infringe upon the free will of others. Instead, focus on spells that promote healing, personal growth, and positive transformation.
- o Ensure that your intentions are rooted in love, compassion, and respect for all beings. Use your candle magic to bring about harmony, balance, and empowerment.

4. Responsible Spellcasting:

- o Practice discernment and discern the true motivations behind your spellwork. Reflect on whether your intentions are aligned with the Wiccan Rede and if they promote the greater good.
- o Regularly evaluate and reassess the impact of your spellwork. Take responsibility for any unintended consequences and learn from your experiences.
- o Continuously educate yourself about ethical considerations in spellcasting and seek

guidance from experienced practitioners or mentors.

By embracing the Wiccan Rede in your candle magic practice, you cultivate a sense of mindfulness, empathy, and respect for the interconnected web of life. Remember that the power of candle magic comes with the responsibility to use it wisely and ethically. May your spells always be guided by the intention to harm none and to foster positive change in alignment with the principles of Wicca.

# CONSENT AND FREE WILL IN CANDLE SPELLS

Consent and respect for free will are essential considerations when engaging in candle spells or any form of magic that involves influencing the lives of others. In Wicca, the ethical principles of harming none and honoring personal autonomy guide the approach to spellcasting. Here are some insights into consent and free will in the context of candle spells:

1. Obtaining Consent:

    o When performing candle spells on behalf of others, it is crucial to seek their informed consent. Respect their right to make their own choices and decisions.

    o Explain the nature of the spell, its intended purpose, and any potential outcomes or effects. Allow the person to fully understand and consent to the spellwork before proceeding.

- If someone expresses discomfort or declines your offer to perform a candle spell, honor their wishes and refrain from proceeding. Consent should always be freely given.

2. Honoring Free Will:

- Wicca emphasizes the importance of respecting the free will of individuals. It is essential to avoid manipulating or coercing others through candle magic.
- Do not use candle spells to force someone to act against their own desires or to infringe upon their autonomy. Instead, focus on spells that empower and support their personal growth and well-being.
- Recognize that everyone has their own unique journey and lessons to learn. Allow individuals the freedom to make their own choices and face the consequences of those choices.

3. Self-Reflection and Intentions:

o Before casting a candle spell, reflect on your own intentions and motivations. Ensure that they align with the principles of consent, free will, and the highest good for all involved.

o Ask yourself if your spellwork respects the autonomy and well-being of others. Consider whether there are alternative ways to achieve your desired outcomes that do not involve influencing the lives of others without their consent.

4. Ethical Considerations:

o Consider the potential consequences and ethical implications of your candle spells. Reflect on how they may impact the lives of others and whether they align with the principles of harm none and personal autonomy.

o Avoid using candle spells to manipulate or control others, as this goes against the principles of consent and free will. Instead, focus on spells that promote healing, positive transformation, and personal empowerment.

5. Responsible Practice:

- Continuously educate yourself about ethical considerations in spellcasting and seek guidance from experienced practitioners or mentors.
- Regularly evaluate and reassess your own ethical framework. Reflect on the impact of your spellwork and learn from any unintended consequences or ethical dilemmas that arise.

By approaching candle spells with a deep respect for consent and free will, you demonstrate a commitment to ethical practice in Wicca. Remember that the true power of magic lies in fostering positive change while honoring the autonomy and well-being of all involved. May your candle spells be guided by a deep sense of respect, consent, and the highest good for all.

# KARMIC CONSIDERATIONS AND RESPONSIBILITY

In Wicca, the concept of karma and personal responsibility plays a significant role in spellcasting and magical practices. Understanding karmic considerations and taking responsibility for your actions can help ensure that your candle spells align with the principles of Wicca. Here are some insights into karmic considerations and personal responsibility in candle magic:

1. The Law of Threefold Return:

   o The Law of Threefold Return is a belief that whatever energy or actions you send out into the world, whether through spellwork or everyday life, will return to you three-fold.

   o When performing candle spells, be mindful of the intentions and energies you are directing. Ensure that they are positive, ethical, and in alignment with the principles of Wicca.

o Remember that the energy you put into your candle spells has the potential to manifest and come back to you, so always consider the consequences and impact of your actions.

2. Ethical Decision-Making:

o Before casting a candle spell, take time to reflect on the ethical implications of your intentions and the potential effects they may have on others.

o Consider the Wiccan Rede and its emphasis on harm none. Ensure that your spellwork promotes positive change, respects the free will of others, and aligns with the principles of personal responsibility.

o Evaluate the motivations behind your spellwork and strive to act from a place of love, compassion, and integrity.

3. Personal Reflection and Growth:

o Engage in regular self-reflection to assess your own beliefs, values, and actions. Consider how they align with the principles of Wicca and how they may contribute to your karmic journey.

o Take responsibility for the consequences of your actions, both intended and unintended. Learn from your experiences, and strive to grow and evolve as a practitioner.

4. Harm and Healing:

o Be mindful of the potential harm that can be caused by candle spells. Avoid using magic for manipulative or harmful purposes.

o Focus on spells that promote healing, personal growth, and positive transformation. Use your candle magic to bring about balance, harmony, and well-being for yourself and others.

5. Gratitude and Appreciation:

o Cultivate a sense of gratitude and appreciation for the gifts of the Universe and the opportunities to practice magic. Recognize the interconnectedness of all beings and the responsibility that comes with wielding magical energy.

6. Seeking Guidance:

   ○ Seek guidance from experienced practition-
     ers or mentors to deepen your understand-
     ing of karmic considerations and personal
     responsibility in candle magic.
   ○ Engage in ongoing learning and self-study
     to enhance your knowledge and ethical
     practice.

By considering karmic implications and taking responsibility for your actions, you can ensure that your
candle spells are aligned with the principles of Wicca
and contribute to your spiritual growth. Embrace the
journey of personal responsibility and learn from the
lessons that arise from your magical practices. May
your candle spells be guided by integrity, compassion, and a deep understanding of the interconnectedness of all things.

# BALANCING PERSONAL DESIRES WITH THE GREATER GOOD

I n the practice of candle magic, it is important to strike a balance between pursuing personal desires and considering the greater good. Wicca emphasizes the interconnectedness of all beings and the responsibility to act in harmony with the natural world. Here are some insights into balancing personal desires with the greater good in candle spellcasting:

1. Self-Reflection and Intention:

   o Before casting a candle spell, engage in self-reflection to understand your motivations and desires. Consider whether they align with the principles of Wicca and the greater good.

o Examine the potential impact of your spellwork on others and the environment. Evaluate whether it serves a self-serving purpose or contributes to the well-being and harmony of all involved.

2. Ethical Decision-Making:

o Make ethical decisions by considering the consequences of your actions. Evaluate whether your desires align with the principles of harm none and respect for the autonomy of others.

o Reflect on whether there are alternative ways to achieve your desires that are more aligned with the greater good and do not harm or infringe upon others.

3. Collaborative and Harmonious Approaches:

o Consider collaborating with others in your spellwork to promote a sense of unity and shared intentions. This can foster a collective focus on the greater good rather than solely individual desires.

o Seek to create harmony and balance in your spellcasting, taking into account the interconnectedness of all beings. Aim for out-comes that benefit not just yourself, but also the community and the natural world.

4. Responsible Use of Power:

o Recognize the power you hold as a practi-tioner of candle magic and use it responsi-bly. Avoid using magic to manipulate or control others for personal gain.

o Instead, focus on spells that promote heal-ing, personal growth, and positive trans-formation. Use your candle magic to em-power yourself and others in ways that are aligned with the greater good.

5. Gratitude and Service:

o Cultivate a sense of gratitude for the gifts and abundance in your life. Use your spellwork to express gratitude and to serve others in need.

o Consider how your desires and spellwork can contribute to the well-being of the community, the Earth, and future genera-tions. Strive to leave a positive and sustain-able impact.

6. Continual Learning and Growth:

- Engage in ongoing learning and self-reflection to deepen your understanding of the interconnectedness of all things. Seek wisdom from experienced practitioners and study the teachings of Wicca.
- Embrace the process of personal growth and transformation as you navigate the delicate balance between personal desires and the greater good.

By consciously balancing personal desires with the greater good, you align your candle spellcasting with the principles of Wicca. Embrace a mindset of unity, responsibility, and service to create positive change that extends beyond yourself. May your spellwork be guided by wisdom, compassion, and a deep respect for the interconnectedness of all beings.

# EMBRACING THE MAGIC OF CANDLE SPELLS

C andle spells are a powerful and enchanting form of magic within the realm of Wicca. They harness the energy of fire, the flickering flame representing the transformation and manifestation of intentions. Embracing the magic of candle spells allows you to tap into your inner power and connect with the energies of the universe. Here are some key aspects to consider when immersing yourself in the magic of candle spells:

1. Setting Intentions:

   o Before engaging in a candle spell, take time to clearly define your intention. Clarify what you seek to manifest or transform through your spellwork. This intention will serve as the guiding force behind your magical practice.

2. Creating Sacred Space:

   o Establish a sacred space for your candle spells. This can be a quiet corner of your home, a personal altar, or any space where you feel connected to the divine. Clear the space of any negative energies and imbue them with love and positive vibrations.

3. Ritual and Ceremony:

   o Engage in rituals and ceremonies that enhance the sacredness of your candle spells. This may include lighting candles, chanting incantations or affirmations, using specific gestures or movements, and incorporating symbolic objects or tools.

4. Visualization and Focus:

   o Visualize your intention as clearly as possible while focusing your energy and attention on the flame of the candle. See your desires manifesting and feel the energy building within you. Concentrate your thoughts and emotions on your desired outcome.

5. Timing and Astrological Considerations:

o Consider the timing of your candle spells. Some practitioners align their spells with specific lunar phases, planetary alignments, or seasonal energies to enhance the potency of their intentions. Explore the influence of celestial bodies on your magical practice.

6. Personalizing Your Spells:

o Infuse your candle spells with personal touches that resonate with you. Add herbs, oils, crystals, or symbols that correspond to your intention. Customize your spells to align with your unique connection to the elements and your personal spiritual path.

7. Trusting Your Intuition:

o Cultivate a deep trust in your intuition as you work with candle spells. Listen to your inner voice, as it will guide you in making choices that are aligned with your highest good and the flow of universal energy.

8. Gratitude and Release:

- Express gratitude for the magic of candle spells and the energies you have invoked. Release your attachment to the outcome and surrender to the divine timing and wisdom of the universe. Trust that your intentions have been heard and will manifest in the most appropriate way.

9. Learning and Growing:

- Embrace a lifelong journey of learning and growing in your practice of candle magic. Seek knowledge from books, mentors, and other practitioners. Experiment with different techniques and observe the results to deepen your understanding of the magic within you.

10. Ethical Considerations:

- Always uphold the ethical principles of Wicca, such as harm none and respect for free will, in your candle spells. Use your magic responsibly, with a compassionate and loving heart, ensuring that your intentions are aligned with the highest good for all involved.

By embracing the magic of candle spells, you tap into the limitless power within yourself and the universe. Allow the flames of your candles to illuminate your path, guide your intentions, and bring forth the manifestation of your desires. Embrace the enchantment, wonder, and transformative nature of candle magic in your spiritual journey. May your candle spells be filled with love, light, and the profound magic that resides within you.

# CONTINUING YOUR JOURNEY IN WICCAN CANDLE MAGIC

Embarking on a journey in Wiccan candle magic is an ongoing process of learning, growth, and deepening your connection to the mystical world. As you continue on this path, there are several important aspects to consider that will enrich your practice and expand your understanding of Wiccan candle magic. Here are some key points to guide you as you continue your journey:

1. Further Study and Exploration:

    o Continue to study and explore the rich history, traditions, and teachings of Wicca and candle magic. Dive into books, online resources, and join communities where you can connect with like-minded individuals and expand your knowledge.

2. Personal Reflection and Journaling:

o Engage in regular personal reflection and journaling to deepen your understanding of your own spiritual journey and experiences with candle magic. Take note of the spells you perform, the results you observe, and any insights or messages received during your practice.

3. Connecting with Nature:

o Strengthen your connection to nature, as it is the foundation of Wicca. Spend time outdoors, and observe the cycles of the moon, the changing seasons, and the elements. Incorporate elements from nature, such as flowers, leaves, or natural materials, into your candle spells.

4. Building Your Magical Toolkit:

o Expand your collection of magical tools and supplies to enhance your candle spells. Acquire herbs, crystals, essential oils, and other correspondences that align with your intentions. Use these tools to amplify the energy and symbolism in your rituals.

5. Developing Your Intuitive Abilities:

o Cultivate your intuition and psychic abilities to deepen your connection with the spiritual realm. Practice meditation, energy work, divination, or any other techniques that resonate with you. Trust your inner wisdom as you work with candle magic.

6. Ritual Crafting and Spell Design:

o Explore the art of ritual crafting and spell design. Experiment with creating your own rituals and spells, infusing them with your unique intentions, symbols, and correspondences. Allow your creativity to flow as you tailor your practice to align with your personal journey.

7. Exploring Advanced Techniques:

o Once you have developed a solid foundation, consider exploring more advanced techniques in candle magic. This may include working with planetary energies, elemental invocations, or advanced spellcasting methods. Always approach advanced techniques with respect and caution.

8. Ritual Ethics and Responsibility:

o  Continually evaluate and uphold the ethical principles of Wicca in your candle magic practice. Reflect on the consequences of your actions, ensuring they align with the Wiccan Rede and the principles of harm none. Take responsibility for the energy you channel and the intentions you set.

9. Connecting with Community:

o  Seek opportunities to connect with fellow Wiccans and practitioners of candle magic. Attend workshops, festivals, or online communities where you can share experiences, exchange knowledge, and find support on your journey. Engaging with others can provide valuable insights and deepen your practice.

10. Embracing Your Unique Path:

- Remember that each practitioner's path is unique. Embrace your individuality and trust your own intuition and guidance. Your journey in Wiccan candle magic is a personal exploration that evolves and unfolds in its own time and in accordance with your spiritual growth.

By continuing your journey in Wiccan candle magic with an open heart and a thirst for knowledge, you will discover new depths of wisdom and connection. Embrace the opportunities for growth, celebrate your successes, and learn from any challenges along the way. May your path be illuminated by the flame of knowledge and guided by the loving energies of the universe.

# GRATITUDE AND CLOSING THE CIRCLE

As you conclude your candle magic rituals and spellwork, it is important to express gratitude and properly close the circle. This final step allows you to honor the energies you have invoked, release any remaining energy, and bring your practice to a harmonious conclusion. Here are some key elements to consider when expressing gratitude and closing the circle:

1. Expressing Gratitude:

   o Take a moment to express gratitude for the energies, deities, spirits, or elements you have worked with during your candle magic practice. Offer thanks for their presence, guidance, and support throughout your ritual.

2. Release and Grounding:

○ Visualize any remaining energy that you have raised or accumulated during your spellwork flowing back into the Earth. Feel yourself becoming grounded and connected to the physical realm. This process ensures that any excess energy is released and dispersed.

3. Thanking Your Tools:

○ Express gratitude to the tools and materials you have used in your candle magic practice. Acknowledge the contributions they have made to your rituals and the energy they have helped to channel. This can include thanking your candles, herbs, oils, crystals, and any other items you have utilized.

4. Closing Affirmations:

○ Recite closing affirmations or prayers to formally close the circle. This can be a simple statement of gratitude, such as "I thank the energies that have been present and now release them with love and gratitude. The circle is now closed."

5.  Extinguishing the Candles:

    o  Safely extinguish the candles used in your ritual, either by snuffing them out or letting them burn down completely. As you do so, express gratitude for the transformative power of the flame and the manifestation of your intentions.

6.  Grounding and Centering:

    o  Take a few moments to ground yourself and bring your energy back to a centered state. You can do this through deep breathing, visualization, or any other grounding technique that resonates with you. Feel yourself rooted in the present moment and connected to the Earth.

7.  Reflection and Integration:

    o  After closing the circle, take time to reflect on your experiences and the results of your candle magic. Journal any insights, feelings, or synchronicities that occurred during your practice. This reflection allows for deeper integration of the magic and lessons learned.

Remember, closing the circle is an important step in bringing your candle magic practice to a balanced conclusion. It helps to maintain energetic boundaries, express gratitude, and ensure a harmonious completion of your rituals. Embrace this closing process with mindfulness, reverence, and appreciation for the magical experiences you have had. May your practice be infused with gratitude, love, and the transformative power of candle magic.

# CORRESPONDENCE TABLES FOR CANDLE COLORS, HERBS, AND OILS

When working with candle magic, the selection of colors, herbs, and oils can greatly enhance and focus the energy of your spells. The following tables provide a general guide to the correspondences associated with various candle colors, herbs, and oils commonly used in Wiccan candle magic. However, it's important to remember that personal intuition and preference should always be taken into account when selecting correspondences for your specific intentions.

1. Candle Color Correspondences:

   o White: Purity, spirituality, healing, protection, clarity, new beginnings.

- Red: Passion, love, courage, strength, vitality, power, sexuality.
- Pink: Romantic love, self-love, friendship, harmony, compassion.
- Orange: Creativity, success, joy, enthusiasm, attraction, motivation.
- Yellow: Intellect, communication, confidence, mental clarity, inspiration.
- Green: Abundance, prosperity, fertility, growth, healing, harmony.
- Blue: Peace, tranquility, intuition, spiritual guidance, healing, wisdom.
- Purple: Psychic abilities, spirituality, intuition, divination, meditation.
- Black: Protection, banishing negativity, breaking bad habits, releasing.
- Silver: Intuition, psychic development, feminine energy, lunar magic.
- Gold: Abundance, success, wealth, prosperity, masculine energy, solar magic.

2. Herb Correspondences:

- Lavender: Calming, peace, purification, sleep, spiritual healing.
- Rosemary: Protection, clarity, memory, concentration, purification.

- Sage: Cleansing, wisdom, clarity, removing negativity, spiritual connection.
- Chamomile: Soothing, relaxation, peace, healing, sleep, prosperity.
- Cinnamon: Energy, passion, love, prosperity, success, courage.
- Frankincense: Spirituality, purification, meditation, spiritual growth.
- Patchouli: Grounding, prosperity, love, passion, spiritual growth.
- Rose: Love, romance, emotional healing, self-love, beauty.
- Bay Leaves: Protection, divination, success, wishes, psychic powers.
- Mugwort: Psychic abilities, lucid dreaming, divination, protection.

3. Oil Correspondences:

- Sandalwood: Spirituality, meditation, healing, grounding, protection.
- Rose: Love, romance, emotional healing, self-love, attracting love.
- Lavender: Calming, relaxation, peace, purification, sleep.
- Patchouli: Grounding, prosperity, love, passion, spiritual growth.

- ○ Frankincense: Spirituality, purification, meditation, spiritual growth.
- ○ Citrus: Energy, happiness, clarity, uplifting, purification.
- ○ Jasmine: Love, sensuality, emotional healing, attracting positive energy.
- ○ Eucalyptus: Healing, purification, clearing energy, invigorating.
- ○ Cedarwood: Protection, grounding, wisdom, attracting abundance.
- ○ Peppermint: Energy, clarity, focus, purification, invigorating.

Remember, these correspondences are not set in stone and can vary based on personal associations, cultural backgrounds, and individual preferences. It's essential to trust your intuition and select correspondences that resonate with your intentions and personal connection to the elements. Experiment, observe the results, and adjust as needed to create a powerful and personalized candle magic practice.

# GLOSSARY OF WICCAN TERMS

To help you navigate the terminology commonly used in Wicca, here is a glossary of Wiccan terms:

1. Wicca: A modern pagan religious movement that encompasses various traditions and practices centered around nature worship, magic, and reverence for the divine.

2. Witch: A practitioner of witchcraft and magic. In Wicca, the terms "witch" and "Wiccan" are often used interchangeably.

3. Coven: A group of Witches or Wiccans who gather together for rituals, celebrations, and magical workings. Covens are often led by a High Priestess or High Priest.

4. Ritual: A formalized set of actions, prayers, and gestures performed in a sacred space to create

a connection with the divine, perform magic, or celebrate specific occasions.

5. Book of Shadows: A personal journal or grimoire used by Wiccans and witches to record rituals, spells, correspondences, and personal reflections. It serves as a repository of magical knowledge and experiences.

6. Altar: A dedicated space used for rituals and magical workings. It typically includes items such as candles, symbols, tools, and representations of the elements.

7. Elements: Earth, Air, Fire, Water, and Spirit. These elemental energies are often invoked and honored in Wiccan rituals, symbolizing different aspects of nature and spiritual forces.

8. Sabbats: Eight seasonal celebrations that mark significant points in the Wiccan Wheel of the Year, such as Samhain, Yule, Imbolc, Ostara, Beltane, Litha, Lammas, and Mabon. They honor the cycles of nature and reflect upon the changing seasons.

9. Esbats: Rituals held during the full moon, which provide opportunities for magic, divination, and connecting with lunar energies.

10. Athame: A ceremonial knife with a double-edged blade, often used to direct and focus en-

ergy during rituals. It symbolizes the element of Air and is associated with the masculine divine energy.

11. Chalice: A ritual cup representing the element of Water and the feminine divine energy. It is often used to hold ritual beverages such as water or wine.

12. Pentacle: A five-pointed star enclosed in a circle. It symbolizes the five elements and is often used as a representation of protection and sacred space.

13. Casting the Circle: The act of creating a sacred space by visualizing and energetically enclosing an area for magical workings and rituals. It serves as a boundary between the mundane world and the spiritual realm.

14. Goddess: The feminine divine principle in Wicca, representing aspects such as fertility, nurturing, intuition, and the cycles of life.

15. God: The masculine divine principle in Wicca, representing aspects such as strength, vitality, protection, and the cycles of nature.

16. Magic: The practice of harnessing and directing natural energies to create change or manifest desires. It involves working with symbols, rituals, and personal intention.

17. Ancestor: A deceased family member or loved one who is honored and revered in Wiccan traditions. Ancestors are often called upon for guidance, protection, and ancestral connections.
18. Divination: The practice of seeking knowledge or insight about the future or hidden truths through tools such as tarot cards, runes, scrying, or other forms of psychic exploration.
19. Grounding: The process of connecting with the Earth's energy to release excess energy and restore balance. It involves visualizing roots extending into the ground or physical actions like walking barefoot on the Earth.
20. Sabbatical: A period of intentional rest, reflection, and study taken by some Wiccans or witches to deepen their spiritual practice and recharge their energy.

This glossary provides a starting point for understanding key terms used in Wicca. Keep in mind that different traditions and practitioners may have their own variations and interpretations. Continually explore and learn, allowing your own experiences to shape your understanding of these terms within your personal Wiccan journey.

# THANK YOU

T hank You for Exploring the Magic of Candle Spells.

As you reach the end of this book on Wiccan candle spells, we extend our heartfelt gratitude for embarking on this journey of magical exploration. Throughout these pages, we have delved into the enchanting world of candle magic, uncovering its history, techniques, and profound significance within the practice of Wicca.

From the power of candle magic and its ability to manifest intentions to the ethical considerations, correspondences, and rituals involved, you have gained a comprehensive understanding of this ancient art. We have explored the various types of spells, from love and attraction to protection and banishing, healing and wellness to prosperity and abundance, and divination to psychic enhancement. Additionally, we have embraced the sacred cycles of the moon, the elements, ancestral connections, and the celebration of seasonal rituals.

You have learned how to create a sacred space, choose ritual tools, consider timing and astrological influences, cast circles, and personalize your candle spells. The importance of intention, symbolism, and visualization has been emphasized, along with ethical guidelines, consent, and the balance between personal desires and the greater good.

We have provided you with a comprehensive glossary of Wiccan terms, correspondence tables for colors, herbs, and oils, and a list of recommended reading and resources to continue your study and deepen your practice. Whether you are a beginner or an experienced practitioner, this book aimed to inspire and empower you on your path.

As you incorporate the wisdom gained from these pages into your own magical journey, remember to approach your practice with reverence, respect, and responsibility. Embrace the power of candle spells to create positive change in your life and the lives of others, while always honoring the principles of the Wiccan Rede.

May your candle flames burn brightly, illuminating your path and connecting you to the divine energies that surround us. Thank you for joining us on this enchanting exploration of Wiccan candle magic. May it bring you joy, growth, and profound spiritual connections.

Blessed be.